ASVAB AFQT
CRASH COURSE®

By Wallie Walker-Hammond

 Research & Education Association
Visit our website at: www.rea.com

Research & Education Association
61 Ethel Road West
Piscataway, New Jersey 08854
E-mail: info@rea.com

ASVAB AFQT CRASH COURSE®

Published 2015
Copyright © 2012 by Research & Education Association, Inc.
All rights reserved. No part of this book may be reproduced
in any form without permission of the publisher.

Printed in the United States of America

Library of Congress Control Number 2011929822

ISBN-13: 978-0-7386-0904-1
ISBN-10: 0-7386-0904-8

 Crash Course® and REA® are registered trademarks of
Research & Education Association, Inc.

TABLE of CONTENTS

CHAPTERS

Foreword

Now that you have accepted the challenge to take up arms and defend your country, you have to pass the first of many tests you will face before you can wear the uniform of our country's armed forces with pride.

Some of you have struggled through high school wishing you could have had a little more help getting through those tests. Others wish they could have had a practice test or two before taking on the real one.

REA's *ASVAB AFQT Crash Course* is the real deal. By studying this book you will get the edge you're looking for. The ASVAB is not something to be taken lightly. Your military career depends on your doing well. REA's book will introduce you, step by step, challenge by challenge, to the one test that will determine the career path you will follow. It is the difference between getting by and doing well.

It's your challenge. It's your future. It's your career. Study REA's *ASVAB AFQT Crash Course* and you will be prepared to face that challenge without any worry about the outcome.

Let me be the first to congratulate you on your chosen service. Study hard—REA will help you succeed.

Peter F. Sheridan, MT2/SS
Missile Technician Second Class
Qualified Submarines
United States Navy

About This Book

Congratulations on your decision to enlist in the military! Choosing to serve your country is a rewarding tradition, and we want to help you reach your military goals. Getting a high score on the ASVAB AFQT is an important first step toward joining the Armed Services. Whether you have a few days, a couple of weeks, or several months to study for the AFQT, this Crash Course system will prepare you for the exam.

REA's *ASVAB AFQT Crash Course* is a targeted test prep designed to assist you in getting the score you need on the Armed Forces Qualifying Test (AFQT). This book was developed based on an in-depth analysis of the Armed Services Vocational Aptitude Battery (ASVAB), the larger test your AFQT score will be taken from.

Written by the author of REA's highly regarded *Your Total ASVAB Solution*, our easy-to-read format covers everything you need to know for the ASVAB AFQT. Our breakthrough study method helps you get a higher score in less time. How? It's simple.

Unlike other test preps, REA's *ASVAB AFQT Crash Course* gives you a review that specifically targets the material tested on the exam. The four chapters that make up the *Crash Course* cover each of the four sections of the AFQT: word knowledge, paragraph comprehension, mathematics knowledge, and arithmetic reasoning. In each chapter, we teach the content and then provide exercises along with a mini-practice test, complete with detailed answer explanations.

After you work through the chapters, take the full-length AFQT practice test in the book. Review all the answers and note where you missed questions. This practice test will give you a solid idea of how you will do on the real AFQT. Do you have the score you need? If not, review the chapters or sections where you answered questions incorrectly and see where you can improve your skills.

To check your test readiness for the ASVAB, either before or after studying this *Crash Course*, take our online practice exam at *www.rea.com/studycenter*. This true-to-format test features automatic scoring, detailed answer explanations, and diagnostic feedback to help you identify your strengths and weaknesses, so you'll be ready on exam day!

No matter how or when you prepare for the AFQT, REA's *Crash Course* will show you how to study efficiently and strategically, so you can get the score you need.

A high score on the AFQT will increase your potential career options. If you're unsure about which military career might be the right fit for you, read over our listing of Military Occupation Specialties in Chapter 6.

Good luck on the AFQT!

ABOUT THE AUTHOR

Wallie Walker-Hammond is the author of REA's acclaimed *Your Total ASVAB Solution* as well as REA's *U.S. Postal Exams 473/473c*. She is also author or editor of more than 65 other test-preparation titles. Her extensive experience in testing includes more than 20 years as an assessment specialist at Educational Testing Service.

ACKNOWLEDGMENTS

In addition to our author, we would like to thank Larry B. Kling, Vice President, Editorial, for his overall direction; Pam Weston, Publisher, for setting the quality standards for production integrity and managing the publication to completion; Michael Reynolds, Managing Editor, for project management; Weymouth Design, for designing our cover; and S4Carlisle Publishing Services, for typesetting this edition.

Introduction

BE ALL YOU CAN BE! THE FEW. THE PROUD. CROSS INTO THE BLUE! ACCELERATE YOUR LIFE!

The Armed Forces Qualifying Test, or AFQT, is not one test. It is actually a subset of the Armed Forces Vocational Aptitude Battery, or ASVAB. The AFQT score is the primary score that gets you into the military. Each branch of the military has its own minimum AFQT score that determines your military fitness. This book will help you achieve the score you need, no matter whether it is for the Army, Air Force, Navy, Coast Guard, or Marines!

SEMPER PARATUS (ALWAYS READY)

Much of what is on the AFQT is material you've already covered in your high school classes. We'll give you the basics and reinforce those basics with drills, exercises, and a practice test that you'll find at the end of the book. We designed this book with you in mind—the potential recruit who wants to enlist. What you'll find ahead of you here is everything you need and nothing more. Once you get into the military, the scores on the other subsets of the ASVAB determine which jobs you may be well suited for. But remember, if you don't meet a certain minimum score on the subtests that make up the AFQT (see above), you won't even be able to enlist. We are here to help you.

A full-length ASVAB practice test is available online at *www.rea.com/studycenter*.

THIS WE'LL DEFEND: HOW THIS BOOK IS ORGANIZED

Chapter 1: What Is the ASVAB AFQT?

This chapter provides you with everything you need to know about the ASVAB and the AFQT. There is information about the origins of the ASVAB and the test's content. You'll also find some test-taking strategies and scoring information.

Chapter 2: Word Knowledge

With this chapter, we begin the review and practice for which REA is noted. The Word Knowledge section of the test asks you to choose the correct definition of words. We present you with the vocabulary skills you need, including plenty of practice using those skills.

Chapter 3: Paragraph Comprehension

This chapter not only gives you the skills you need to do well, it also gives you the strategies you need to be a more *active* reader, no matter what you like to read.

Chapter 4: Mathematics Knowledge

This chapter covers the mathematical concepts that are included on the test. It also gives you a clear picture of the techniques needed to handle each question type effectively.

Chapter 5: Arithmetic Reasoning

Arithmetic reasoning is another way to say "word problems." These word problems cover everyday situations while measuring your reasoning skills.

Chapter 6: What Job Do You Really Want?

This chapter provides a list of Military Occupation Specialties (MOS) that will give you an idea of some of the positions available in the Armed Services. There are lots of occupations and this is your chance to browse through your options and decide what interests you.

ABOVE ALL

You don't have to read this book from cover to cover, but we hope that you will. Don't let its small size fool you—we've designed it to be user-friendly and chock-full of useful information and practice to "be all it can be" just for you. Just remember that practice and preparation will get you where you want to go. REA is with you all the way.

We wish you luck on your journey.

What Is the ASVAB AFQT?

What We'll Cover in This Chapter

- ASVAB Basics
- AFQT Basics
- Test-Taking Strategies

By studying this book, you can achieve a top score on the ASVAB AFQT. The ASVAB assesses knowledge that you've gained throughout your high school career. Most of the knowledge tested on the ASVAB (Armed Forces Vocational Aptitude Battery) is covered in your high school classes.

ABOUT THE ASVAB

You can take the ASVAB as early as your sophomore year in high school, but if you take the ASVAB as a sophomore your score will not be used for joining the military. If you have to take the ASVAB again, you can retake the test after 30 days, and again 30 days later.

The ASVAB, which is developed and maintained by the U.S. Department of Defense, is given at more than 14,000 schools and Military Entrance Processing Stations (MEPS) nationwide. It is also the most widely used multiple-aptitude test battery in the world. The ASVAB is required by the Armed Forces for new recruits joining one of the branches of the military following high school. The scores aid in placing recruits into military jobs. The scores are also helpful, but not a requirement, in choosing an academic or vocational plan after you graduate from high school.

> *The ASVAB was originally designed to predict future academic and occupational success in military occupations. From the time the ASVAB was introduced in 1968, studies have reported that the ASVAB does what it was designed to do.*

Once you take the test, you and your guidance counselor or your recruiter will receive a written report that analyzes your test scores and explains in what fields you might excel based not only on the test scores but on the type of interests and lifestyle you wish to pursue.

If you have a question about your scores, you can contact your local military recruiting office or speak to your guidance counselor.

Test Tip

> *There's no pass or fail on the ASVAB. You can't "beat" it or "flunk" it, and ASVAB scores are good for 2 years.*

ASVAB AND AFQT TEST CONTENT

The ASVAB contains eight, nine, or ten subtests (or sections), depending upon which version of the ASVAB you take, each of which is individually scored. The Armed Forces Qualifying Test (AFQT) is not a single test. It is a composite of four core tests that measure knowledge based on typical high school courses. The four core tests give one overall score and that score is used by the Army, Navy, Marines, Air Force, and Coast Guard to assess how qualified new recruits are. Your scores in four critical areas—Arithmetic Reasoning, Word Knowledge, Paragraph Comprehension, and Mathematics Knowledge—count toward your Armed Forces Qualifying Test (AFQT) score. Keep in mind that the AFQT score determines whether you're qualified to enlist in the military. Your scores on the other subtests will determine how qualified you are for certain military occupational specialties.

THE FOUR ASVAB SUBTESTS THAT MAKE UP THE AFQT

Here is a more detailed description of each of the subtests that make up the AFQT.

ARITHMETIC REASONING

The Arithmetic Reasoning subtest has 30 word problems that focus on everyday life situations. It tests operations with whole numbers, fractions and decimals, ratios and proportions, interest and percentage, as well as measurement.

WORD KNOWLEDGE

The Word Knowledge subtest has 35 questions that ask you to choose the correct definition of words. There are two types of Word Knowledge questions: words that are presented alone and words that are presented in the context of a short sentence.

PARAGRAPH COMPREHENSION

The Paragraph Comprehension subtest has 15 questions that are based on short passages. The passages come from a variety of sources and are about various topics. The questions will test literal comprehension and inference. The literal comprehension questions test your ability to identify facts, and the inference questions test your ability to draw conclusions, identify main ideas, and determine the purpose of the passage.

MATHEMATICS KNOWLEDGE

The Mathematics Knowledge subtest has 25 questions that test your knowledge of math concepts and basic math principles. You'll find questions on numbers (factors, multiples, properties, integers), numeration (fractions, decimals, percents, order of operations, rounding, roots and radicals), algebra (solving equations, simplifying algebraic expressions, factoring), geometry (coordinates, slope, angles, perimeter, area, volume), and probability.

VERSIONS OF THE ASVAB

There are three versions of the ASVAB:

MET-Site ASVAB: Paper-and-pencil test administered by military recruiters at a satellite test site.

CAT-ASVAB: Computer-adaptive test administered by military recruiters at a Military Entrance Processing Station (MEPS).

Student ASVAB: Paper-and-pencil test administered in high school.

The following chart shows you the subtests we just mentioned and gives a brief description of each, as well as the time allowed and the number of questions.

MET-Site Paper and Pencil Administration

Tested on AFQT?	9 Subtests	Minutes	Questions	Description
No	General Science (GS)	11	25	Measures knowledge of life science, earth and space science, and physical science.
Yes	Arithmetic Reasoning (AR)	36	30	Measures ability to solve basic math problems.
Yes	Word Knowledge (WK)	11	35	Measures ability to understand the meaning of words through synonyms.
Yes	Paragraph Comprehension (PC)	13	15	Measures ability to obtain information from written materials.
Yes	Mathematics Knowledge (MK)	24	25	Measures knowledge of mathematical concepts and applications.

Continued →

(Continued from previous page)

Tested on AFQT?	9 Subtests	Minutes	Questions	Description
No	Electronics Information (EI)	9	20	Measures knowledge of electrical current, circuits, devices, and electronic systems.
No	Auto & Shop Information (AS)	11	25	Measures knowledge of automotive maintenance and repair and wood and metal shop practices.
No	Mechanical Comprehension (MC)	19	25	Measures knowledge of the principles of mechanical devices, structural support, and properties of materials.
No	Assembling Objects (AO)	15	25	Measures spatial and problem-solving activities.
	TOTAL	149	225	

*The items in **bold** count toward the Armed Forces Qualifying Test (AFQT) score.
Source: www.official-asvab.com*

CAT-ASVAB
(Computer-Adaptive Test)

Tested on AFQT?	10 Subtests	Minutes	Questions	Description
No	General Science (GS)	8	16	Measures knowledge of life science, earth and space science, and physical science.

Continued ➝

Tested on AFQT?	10 Subtests	Minutes	Questions	Description
Yes	**Arithmetic Reasoning (AR)**	39	16	Measures ability to solve basic math problems.
Yes	**Word Knowledge (WK)**	8	16	Measures ability to understand the meaning of words through synonyms.
Yes	**Paragraph Comprehension (PC)**	22	11	Measures ability to obtain information from written materials.
Yes	**Mathematics Knowledge (MK)**	18	16	Measures knowledge of mathematical concepts and applications.
No	Electronics Information (EI)	8	16	Measures knowledge of electrical current, circuits, devices, and electronic systems.
No	Auto Information (AI)	6	11	Measures knowledge of automotive maintenance and repair.
No	Shop Information (SI)	5	11	Measures knowledge of wood and metal shop practices.
No	Mechanical Comprehension (MC)	20	16	Measures knowledge of the principles of mechanical devices, structural support, and properties of materials.
No	Assembling Objects (AO)	12	16	Measures spatial and problem-solving activities.
	TOTAL	146	145	

*The items in **bold** count toward the Armed Forces Qualifying Test (AFQT) score.
Source: *www.official-asvab.com*

Student ASVAB
(Career Exploration Program)

Tested on AFQT?	8 Subtests	Minutes	Questions	Description
No	General Science (GS)	11	25	Measures knowledge of life science, earth and space science, and physical science.
Yes	Arithmetic Reasoning (AR)	36	30	Measures ability to solve basic math problems.
Yes	Word Knowledge (WK)	11	35	Measures ability to understand the meaning of words through synonyms.
Yes	Paragraph Comprehension (PC)	13	15	Measures ability to obtain information from written materials.
Yes	Mathematics Knowledge (MK)	24	25	Measures knowledge of mathematical concepts and applications.
No	Electronics Information (EI)	9	20	Measures knowledge of electrical current, circuits, devices, and electronic systems.
No	Auto & Shop Information (AS)	11	25	Measures knowledge of automotive maintenance and repair and wood and metal shop practices.

Continued →

(Continued from previous page)

Tested on AFQT?	8 Subtests	Minutes	Questions	Description
No	Mechanical Comprehension (MC)	19	25	Measures knowledge of the principles of mechanical devices, structural support, and properties of materials.
	TOTAL	134	200	
	ADMIN. TIME	36		
	TOTAL TESTING TIME	170		

*The items in **bold** count toward the Armed Forces Qualifying Test (AFQT) score.
Source: www.official-asvab.com

PAPER-AND-PENCIL ADMINISTRATION

The total time required is 3 to 4 hours, which includes reading the instructions and any other administrative tasks. Each subtest has a fixed number of questions and a time limit. When you complete the questions in a subtest, you may go back to review your answers in that subtest only. When your test is scored, a preliminary Armed Forces Qualifying Test (AFQT) score is usually calculated by the test administrator and made available to your recruiter or counselor immediately after the test session.

Test Tip

The AFQT is comprised of your test results in Arithmetic Reasoning (AR), Math Knowledge (MK), and a Verbal Composite (VE) × 2. Your Verbal Composite score is a combination of your Word Knowledge and Paragraph Comprehension scores.

THE COMPUTERIZED ASVAB: THE COMPUTER ADMINISTRATION

The computerized version of the ASVAB, called the CAT-ASVAB, is an adaptive test. That means that the test adapts to the ability level of each individual. Everyone completes the CAT-ASVAB at his or her own pace. That means when you finish a subtest, you can immediately move to the next subtest without waiting for everyone else in the testing room to finish. There are, however, time limits on each subtest in the CAT-ASVAB. On average, it takes about 1½ hours to complete the CAT-ASVAB. Unlike the paper-and-pencil ASVAB, you will not be able to review or change an answer once you submit it. Your test scores will be available immediately after the testing session.

On the CAT-ASVAB, each test taker starts with a medium-difficulty question. If the test taker answers the question correctly, he or she is given a question that is more difficult. If the test taker answers the question incorrectly, then he or she is given a question that is easier. You can't waste time answering questions that are too difficult or too easy.

The CAT-ASVAB includes a ninth subtest, Assembling Objects, which is designed to measure your strengths and weaknesses in spatial ability. This subtest gauges your ability to visualize three-dimensional puzzle pieces and put them back together after they have been taken apart. As of this printing, this score is used only by the Navy. Please check with your recruiter or guidance counselor for the most up-to-date information about this subtest.

PUTTING IN THE TIME TO REVIEW

This book offers brief subject reviews for each of the subtests that make up the AFQT: Word Knowledge, Paragraph Comprehension, Arithmetic Reasoning, and Mathematics Knowledge. Each review targets the information you'll find most handy to do well on the AFQT portion of the ASVAB. All of the reviews offer practice questions and drills to help you study.

ASVAB TEST-TAKING STRATEGIES

HOW TO BEAT THE CLOCK

Every second counts and you'll want to use the available test time for each subtest in the most efficient way. Here's how.

1. Memorize the directions for each section of the test. You don't want to waste valuable time reading directions on the day of the test. Your time should by spent on answering questions.

2. Bring a watch and pace yourself. Work steadily and quickly. Don't get stuck or spend too much time on any one question. If, after reading the question, you cannot answer it, make a note of it and continue. You can go back to it after you have completed the easier questions first.

3. As you work on the test, be sure that your answers correspond to the proper numbers and letters on the answer sheet.

4. On the paper-and-pencil version, answer every question. If you run out of time, it's to your advantage to fill in random guesses for the remaining questions, since there is no penalty for guessing.

5. On the CAT-ASVAB, if time is running short, try to read and correctly answer the questions, instead of filling in random guesses for the remaining questions. The CAT-ASVAB penalizes you when several incorrect answers are given toward the end of a subtest.

Test Tip

You don't need to have extensive computer experience to take the CAT-ASVAB. The instructions are very clear and concise. The computer keyboard has been modified so that only the keys you need to answer the test questions are labeled. The test administrator will give you keyboard-use instructions on test day.

ABOUT THE SCORING

There is no "right" score on the ASVAB, since this is a test to help you choose a possible career. However, a high score will give you more fields to choose from in the Armed Forces. The scores help military personnel to determine what fields you are best suited for and the fields that may cause some difficulty. Your guidance counselor is trained to interpret your score and give you career advice based on that score.

Each subtest is scored individually. Individual scores are also combined to give you composite scores that show your overall ability. Your *raw score* is calculated using the following formula:

(Word Knowledge score × 2) + (Paragraph Comprehension score × 2) + (Arithmetic Reasoning Score) + (Mathematics Knowledge score)

Three composite scores are calculated as follows:

Verbal Ability Composite = Word Knowledge score + Paragraph Comprehension score

Math Ability Composite = Arithmetic Reasoning score + Mathematics Knowledge score

Academic Ability Composite = Verbal Ability Composite + Math Ability Composite

The composite scores, also known as Career Exploration Scores, are provided to help you explore your career options. They will help you get an idea of your verbal, math and science, and technical skills compared to other students in the same grade. These composite scores can be a valuable tool in helping you map out a career path.

Here are the AFQT qualifying scores for each branch of service:

Army—31

Navy—35

Marines—32

Air Force—36

Coast Guard—36

The scores you receive in the General Science and Auto and Shop Information subtests are not used to calculate any of the composite scores. These scores are used by recruiters and guidance counselors to identify other careers that you may choose to pursue and be successful in.

> *The ASVAB Career Exploration Program provides tools, including the test battery and interest inventory, developed by the Department of Defense to help high school and post-secondary students across the nation learn more about career exploration and planning.*

CHOOSE YOUR CAREER

This book also contains information on military careers. A complete career section, Chapter 6, will allow you to learn about career options inside the military.

Word Knowledge

WHAT TO EXPECT IN THE WORD KNOWLEDGE SECTION OF THE AFQT

The Word Knowledge section is really a vocabulary test and it is one of the most important of the subtests that make up the AFQT. You will need a good score on this section not only to pass the AFQT and be allowed to enlist, you'll also need a good score to qualify for jobs such as military intelligence, air traffic controller, and emergency management specialist, to name a few.

Test Tip

Most people don't have trouble finishing this section since the questions are short. Half of the questions you'll either know or won't know the answers to, while the other half of the questions will provide some context clues.

WORDS TO LIVE BY

The AFQT Word Knowledge section measures your knowledge of synonyms. As you already know, two words are synonyms if they mean the same thing or nearly the same thing. When trying to choose a synonym for a word, you're looking for a word that is *close* in meaning, but not necessarily a word with the exact same definition.

The Word Knowledge section consists of words that are commonly used by people with a high school education.

On this section of the test, you will be given 11 minutes to complete 35 questions. You may not even need the entire 11 minutes since the questions are short and fall into only two types:

- The first type asks you for the definition of a word.

Example:

<u>Reveal</u> most nearly means

    A. defend.

    B. tell.

    C. conceal.

    D. throw.

"Reveal" most nearly means "to say or to tell," so choice (B) is the correct answer.

- The second type gives you a word that's underlined and used in a sentence.

Example:

If you don't have a bike for the Army's triathalon, I can <u>supply</u> one for you to use.

    A. Bring

    B. Remove

    C. Train

    D. Assist

For this type of question, you must choose the answer that is the closest in meaning to the underlined word. In this sentence, "supply" most nearly means "bring," choice (A). For words that are unfamiliar to you, you can use the meaning of the sentence to help you decide which answer choice has the same meaning as the underlined word.

Test Tip

The questions that ask for synonyms ask you to recognize the meaning of the word. If the word is unfamiliar, take it apart—root by root, prefix by prefix, suffix by suffix.

This chapter will help improve your vocabulary knowledge through word parts, word meanings, and drills that will pull together the skills you learned in high school.

DEVELOPING YOUR VOCABULARY

Step one: Read everything. Read books, newspapers, magazines, CD inserts, video game boxes, whatever you want. The more experience you have reading, the more words you'll know.

Step two: Make flashcards. Get some index cards and write down the words you don't know. Use a dictionary and/or a thesaurus to discover the meanings and synonyms of those words and write them down on the back of the flashcards.

Step three: Mentally connect those new words to experiences you've had. Try making sentences using those previously unfamiliar words. If you make those sentences relate to you in some meaningful (get it?) way, you'll learn their synonyms easier and quicker.

Step four: Study roots, suffixes, and prefixes. Studying word parts is an effective way to develop your vocabulary. If you know the root word of an unfamiliar word on the test, you will be able to make an educated guess as to its meaning. (We'll cover word parts soon in this chapter.)

Step five: Work some crossword puzzles. There are lots of crossword puzzles online and in newspapers and magazines that will give you opportunities to practice your word knowledge skills.

Step six: Review the exercises in this chapter. Take this book with you. Review with your friends. Just review. And review. And review.

Which of these do you think will help you build a better vocabulary?

_____ *Read more newspapers and books.*

_____ *Memorize the dictionary.*

_____ *Write down as many words as you can on index cards.*

_____ *Learn word roots, prefixes, and suffixes.*

_____ *Watch lots and lots of television.*

GETTING THE MESSAGE OUT THROUGH WORD PARTS

A great way to figure out what a word means or what word you need to use in your communications is to understand the *parts* of the word. The word parts are *prefixes, suffixes,* and *roots.* The core of the word is called the *root* and the root usually has *prefixes* and *suffixes* around it. Think of the English language as a tree: It has roots, branches, and leaves. Word **roots** are the basic structures that make up words. Many of them have Latin roots, although the English language is a combination of many languages. **Prefixes** are letter combinations that go at the beginning of a word. Look at the word *happy.* If it had the prefix *un-,* which means "not," it becomes *unhappy.* When you see the letters *un* at the beginning of a word, you can figure out that the word's meaning is the *opposite* of whatever the rest of the word means if you take away the letters *un.* Got it? **Suffixes** are easy: They are letter combinations that go at the end of a word. You've seen them: *-ly, -er, -ty, -y.* These are the combinations that help make a word grammatically correct or that sometimes change the meaning of a word.

Prefixes

Prefixes attach themselves to the beginning of a root word either to change its meaning or to create a new word. Here are some common prefixes:

Prefix	Meaning	Example
a-, an-	without	anaerobic—without air
ab-	from, away	absent—away, not present
ad-	to, toward	advance—move toward
ambi- , amphi-	both	ambidextrous—using both hands equally amphibious—living both in water and on land
auto-	self	autobiography—about oneself
bene-, ben-	good, well	benefactor—someone who does good deeds
bi-	two	bicycle—two-wheeled cycle
com-, co-, col-	with, together	cooperate—work with
contra-, contro-	against	contradict—speak against
de-	away from, opposite of	descend—move down detract—draw away from
dia-	across, through	diameter—measurement across

Continued →

(Continued from previous page)

Prefix	Meaning	Example
dis-, di-	not, away from	disagree—not agree dislike—not like
ex-	out of, away from	exhale—breathe out
extra-	beyond, outside	extraterrestrial—beyond the Earth
homo-	same	homonym—sounding the same
hyper-	too much, above	hyperactive—too active
hypo-	too little, under	hypothermia—too little body heat
in-, il-, im-, ir-	not	innocent—not guilty illogical—not logical immature—not mature irresponsible—not responsible
mono-	one, single	monorail—train that runs on one rail
neo-	new	neophyte—rookie
non-	not	nonessential—not essential
peri-	around, near	periscope—scope for seeing all around
poly-	many	polygon—many-sided shape
post-	after, behind	postmortem—after death
pre-	before	preview—view before
pro-	in favor of, in front of	proceed—go in front of
re-	back, again, backward	rewrite—write again retract—take back

Prefix	Meaning	Example
sub-, sus-	under, below	submarine—below the water suspend—hang down
super-	above, over, greater	supervisor—boss
sym-, syn-	together with, at the same time	sympathetic—feeling with
tele-	from a distance, far	telecommute—commuting from a distance
un-	not	unknown—not known
vice-	acting for, next in rank to	vice president—next in rank to the president

Roots

We know that roots constitute the basic element of a word that determines its meaning. A **root** is the main part of a word; prefixes and suffixes may be added to the root. Think about the word *dictionary*. The root is *dict,* which means "to say." A dictionary says what words mean. Since you know what a dictionary is, you might remember the root and use it to figure out other, less familiar words with the same root. Here are some common roots:

Root	Meaning	Example
acr	bitter	acrid
act	do, act	action, react, transact
aero	air	aerospace, aerobics
agr	field	agriculture
alt	high	altitude
audi	hear	auditorium, auditory, audition
bibli	book	bibliography

Continued ➡

(Continued from previous page)

Root	Meaning	Example
bio	life	biosphere, amphibious
brev	short	abbreviation, brevity
capit	head	decapitate, capital
carn	flesh	carnage, carnivorous
cede, ceed, cess	go, yield	recede, precede, exceed, process
cent	hundred	percent, centimeter, centipede
chron	time	chronology, synchronize
cit	summon	cite, excite
civ	citizen	uncivil, civilization
claim, clam	shout, cry out	exclaim, proclaim, clamorous
clar	clear	clarity, declare
cogn	know	cognitive, recognize, incognito
corp	body	corpse
cracy, crat	rule, power	democracy, theocracy, autocratic
cred	trust, believe	credit, incredible
crypt	hidden	cryptic
culp	blame	culprit, culpability
dem	people	demographic, democracy
dent	tooth	dental, indentation
derm	skin	dermatitis
dic, dict	speak	dictation, predict, indicative
dign	worthy	dignified, dignitary

Root	Meaning	Example
doc, doct	teach, prove	doctor, indoctrinate
dorm	sleep	dormitory, dormant
du	two	duo, dual
ego	I	egomania, egotist
fer	carry	transfer, refer, prefer
fuge	flee	refuge, fugitive
geo	earth	geology, geography
gram	something written, recorded	telegram, grammar
graph	to write	graphics, telegraph
hydr	water	dehydration
ject	throw	reject, projection, trajectory
jud	judge	judicial
jur	law	jury, perjure
labor	work	laborious, collaborate
lev	light	levity, alleviate
loc	place	locate, location, locale, allocate
magn	large, great	magnitude, magnificent
mal	bad, ill	malodorous, malingerer
manu	hand	manuscript, manicure, manufacture
mega	large	megaphone, megacycle, megamillion
mill	thousand	millennium
meter	measure	metronome, geometry, barometer
morph	shape, form	amorphous, morphology
mort	death, die	mortify, mortician, mortal

Continued ➡

(Continued from previous page)

Root	Meaning	Example
multi	many	multiply, multinational
nasc, nat	born	native, natural
omni	all	omniscient, omnibus, omnipotent
onym	name	pseudonym
oper	work	operate, cooperation
pater	father	patriot, paternity
ped, pod	foot	pedestrian, impede, tripod
photo	light	photography, photograph
phys	of nature	physical, physics
port	carry	report, portable, deportation
press	press	pressure, impression
psych	of the mind	psychic, psychiatrist
tempor	time	temporary
term	end	terminal, terminate
uni	one	unify, disunity, union
urb	city	urban, suburb
vac	empty	evacuate, vacuous
ver	true	veracity, verity
vers, vert	change	conversion, revert
vid, vis	see	video, television, vision, evidence
vol, volv	roll, turn	involuntary, revolve, evolution
zo	animal	zoologist, Paleozoic

Remember your word branches? Thinking of words in groups is an effective vocabulary-building strategy for the AFQT. It's easier to remember words when you study them in groups of words that have similar meanings.

Suffixes

These parts attach to the end of a root word to change its meaning, form a new word, or sometimes to make the word grammatically correct. Here are some common suffixes:

Suffix	Meaning	Example
-able, -ble	able, capable	likable, acceptable
-ance, -ancy	act or state of	disturbance
-ary, -ar	concerning, relating to	military, polar
-cy	act, state	presidency
-er, -or	someone who/that	presenter, conductor
-fy	to make	pacify
-hood	state, condition	adulthood
-ish	like	foolish, impish
-ism	belief or practice	capitalism, socialism, racism
-ist	someone who does	cyclist, scientist
-ive	of, relating to	destructive
-ize	make into	legalize
-ment	state of being, act of	abandonment, entertainment
-tude	state or quality of	attitude, rectitude
-ward	in the direction of	wayward, homeward

A WORD TO THE WISE

Remember that a word can have a root and a prefix, a root and a suffix, a root and two prefixes, a root and two suffixes, and maybe just a root.

You can try to predict what the meaning is before you look at the answer choices. Many sentences provide a definition of the underlined word.

Attention! Every word must have a root!

Don't worry, we don't expect you to memorize these word parts, but you really should try to figure out their meanings when you see them in words on the test.

WORD BRANCHES

Sometimes it's helpful to think of words as belonging in a particular group or *branch,* that is, words grouped according to their general meaning. We've put together some word groups so you'll see what we mean. Note that not every word is an exact synonym for the others in the group, but each word *is* closely related to the concept that you'll find in the group's heading. These word branches should help you recognize synonyms and words that are related and, to that end, help you further develop your vocabulary.

Add	Aggressive	Appropriate
Acquire	Abrasive	Ethical
Attain	Belligerent	Integrity
Augment	Brutality	
Enhance	Combative	
Procure	Combustion	
	Rude	
	Suppress	

Attractive	Bad	Belief
Aesthetic	Deceit	Confirm
Iridescent	Deceitful	Conviction
Melodious	Malevolent	Justify
Prepossessing	Nefarious	Notion
Radiant	Odious	Precept
Resplendent	Sadistic	
	Traitor	
	Traitorous	
	Underhanded	
	Unscrupulous	

Blame	Bold	Cautious
Culpable	Defiant	Measured
Exculpate	Demagogue	Prudent
Recrimination	Demanding	Reluctant
Scapegoat	Dominant	Tentative
Vindictive	Flagrant	Wary
	Formidable	
	Overpowering	
	Persuasive	
	Provocative	
	Stern	

Clear	Clumsy	Communicate
Clarity	Crass	Allegation
Coherent	Crude	Allege
Disclose	Inept	Assertion
Divulge		Assurance
Explanatory		Commentary
Illustrate		Convey
Transparent		Discourse
		Eulogy
		Extrovert
		Insinuate

Clear	Clumsy	Communicate
Clarity	Bumbling	Irony
Coherent	Cross	Melodrama
Disclose	Gowky	Mutter
Divulge	Inept	Oration
Illustrate	Stumbling	Orator
Lucid	Ungainly	Paraphrase
Obvious	Unwieldly	Proclaim
Transparent		Query
Well-defined		Rhetorical
		Testimony

Continue	Criticize	Decrease
Persevere	Berate	Abate
Persistence	Censure	Abbreviation
Propel	Condemn	Abridge
Reiterate	Condemnation	Alleviate
Repeat	Contempt	Condense
Repetitive	Deride	Curtail
Sequence	Detract	Delete
	Disparage	Deplete
	Impugn	Diminish
	Punitive	Dissipate
	Reprimand	Exhaust
	Taunt	Mitigate
		Withhold

Disagree	Disapprove	Dislike
Contradict	Disapproval	Adversary
Contradiction	Disdain	Adverse
Controversial	Incriminate	Adversity
Discrepancy	Repudiate	
	Scorn	

Disrespect	Encourage	False
Admonish	Endorse	Dubious
Berate	Induce	Erroneous
Debase	Inspire	Fraudulent
Defame	Prod	Illusory
Denigrate	Promote	Fiction
Denounce	Proponent	Forgery
Deride	Stimulate	Fraud
Disparage	Urge	Hypocrisy
Rebuke		Mendacious
Reprimand		Misconception
Reproach		Mythical
Ridicule		Pretense
Scoff		Skepticism
		Specious
		Spurious
		Treachery

Friendly	Good	Happy
Affable	Assiduous	Blissful
Alliance	Benefactor	Content
Ally	Beneficent	Ebullient
Amiable	Benevolent	Ecstatic
Amicable	Empathetic	Effusive
Civility	Equitable	Elated
Congenial	Judicious	Euphoric
Convivial	Magnanimous	Exultant
Cordial	Philanthropic	Jubilant
Felicitous		Jubilation
Genial		Merriment
Gracious		Optimistic
Gregarious		
Humane		
Jocular		
Jovial		
Winsome		

Harmful	Helpful	Hostile
Betray	Accommodate	Antagonist
Calamity	Advantageous	Conflict
Catastrophic	Antidote	Discord
Corrosive	Benign	Divisive
Debacle	Compassion	Inflammatory
Discredit	Complement	Malediction
Exploit	Convenient	Offensive
Hazardous	Nurture	Opponent
Jeopardize	Resource	Parasite
	Solicitous	Ruthless
	Therapeutic	Villain

Lazy	Permanent	Proud
Complacent	Immutable	Boast
Dormant	Pervasive	Boastful
Flaccid	Preservative	Conceit
Indolent	Preserve	Conceited
Lackadaisical		Condescending
Languid		Confident
Lethargic		Egotist
Listless		Exaggerate
Sedentary		Haughty
Slothful		Narcissism
		Smug

Respect	Sad	Strong
Adulate	Condolence	Endurance
Approbate	Consolation	Endure
Extol	Despondent	Enduring
Laud	Doleful	Fortitude
Revere	Forlorn	Paramount
Validate	Inconsolable	Sturdy
Venerate	Melancholy	Tenacious
	Mournful	
	Remorseful	
	Somber	

Time	Weak	
Ancient	Defective	
Archaic	Fragile	
Dated	Impotent	
Duration	Pathetic	
Instantaneous	Untenable	
Interlude		
Longevity		
Nostalgic		
Obsolete		
Outdated		
Periodic		
Punctual		
Timeless		

EXERCISING YOUR VOCABULARY

The following words contain prefixes, roots, and suffixes. Read each word and determine the meaning based on what you know about word parts. Look up each word in the dictionary or a thesaurus and write down a synonym. The first one is done for you.

You may wish to write each term on an index card for ease of use and additional study.

EXERCISE 1

1. **amend**

    Guess: fix   *Word Meaning:* to correct   *Synonym:* improve

2. **diligent**

    Guess: *Word Meaning:*   *Synonym:*

3. **exemplary**

    Guess: *Word Meaning:*   *Synonym:*

4. **critique**

    Guess: *Word Meaning:*   *Synonym:*

Continued →

Exercise 1 (Continued)

5. immune

   Guess: *Word Meaning:*   *Synonym:*

6. palpable

   Guess: *Word Meaning:*   *Synonym:*

7. equitable

   Guess: *Word Meaning:*   *Synonym:*

8. coalition

   Guess: *Word Meaning:*   *Synonym:*

9. elicit

   Guess: *Word Meaning:*   *Synonym:*

10. substandard

   Guess: *Word Meaning:*   *Synonym:*

11. indifferent

   Guess: *Word Meaning:*   *Synonym:*

12. contempt

   Guess: *Word Meaning:*   *Synonym:*

13. conceal

   Guess: *Word Meaning:*   *Synonym:*

14. confirm

   Guess: *Word Meaning:*   *Synonym:*

15. terrestrial

   Guess: *Word Meaning:*   *Synonym:*

16. consensus

   Guess: *Word Meaning:*   *Synonym:*

17. controversy

   Guess: *Word Meaning:*   *Synonym:*

18. demote

   Guess: *Word Meaning:*   *Synonym:*

Continued ➔

Exercise 1 (Continued)

19. malady

Guess: *Word Meaning:*   *Synonym:*

20. illustrious

Guess: *Word Meaning:*   *Synonym:*

21. agrarian

Guess: *Word Meaning:*   *Synonym:*

22. destitute

Guess: *Word Meaning:*   *Synonym:*

23. nocturnal

Guess: *Word Meaning:*   *Synonym:*

24. unyielding

Guess: *Word Meaning:*   *Synonym:*

25. glutton

Guess: *Word Meaning:*   *Synonym:*

26. concise

Guess: *Word Meaning:*   *Synonym:*

EXERCISE 2

1. hypothetical

Guess: *Word Meaning:*   *Synonym:*

2. relegate

Guess: *Word Meaning:*   *Synonym:*

3. susceptible

Guess: *Word Meaning:*   *Synonym:*

4. consternation

Guess: *Word Meaning:*   *Synonym:*

Continued ➙

Exercise 2 (Continued)

5. adulation

   Guess: *Word Meaning:*   *Synonym:*

6. novice

   Guess: *Word Meaning:*   *Synonym:*

7. egregious

   Guess: *Word Meaning:*   *Synonym:*

8. irresolute

   Guess: *Word Meaning:*   *Synonym:*

9. pretentious

   Guess: *Word Meaning:*   *Synonym:*

10. resuscitate

   Guess: *Word Meaning:*   *Synonym:*

11. indifferent

   Guess: *Word Meaning:*   *Synonym:*

12. slovenly

   Guess: *Word Meaning:*   *Synonym:*

13. flagrant

   Guess: *Word Meaning:*   *Synonym:*

14. subsided

   Guess: *Word Meaning:*   *Synonym:*

15. laudable

   Guess: *Word Meaning:*   *Synonym:*

16. astute

   Guess: *Word Meaning:*   *Synonym:*

17. aggravate

   Guess: *Word Meaning:*   *Synonym:*

18. grandiose

   Guess: *Word Meaning:*   *Synonym:*

Continued →

19. censor

Guess:　　　　　　　*Word Meaning:*　　　　　　*Synonym:*

20. antagonist

Guess:　　　　　　　*Word Meaning:*　　　　　　*Synonym:*

21. agnostic

Guess:　　　　　　　*Word Meaning:*　　　　　　*Synonym:*

22. demotion

Guess:　　　　　　　*Word Meaning:*　　　　　　*Synonym:*

23. conspicuous

Guess:　　　　　　　*Word Meaning:*　　　　　　*Synonym:*

24. erroneous

Guess:　　　　　　　*Word Meaning:*　　　　　　*Synonym:*

25. austere

Guess:　　　　　　　*Word Meaning:*　　　　　　*Synonym:*

26. metamorphosis

Guess:　　　　　　　*Word Meaning:*　　　　　　*Synonym:*

EXERCISE 3

1. epithet

Guess:　　　　　　　*Word Meaning:*　　　　　　*Synonym:*

2. mutiny

Guess:　　　　　　　*Word Meaning:*　　　　　　*Synonym:*

3. simulate

Guess:　　　　　　　*Word Meaning:*　　　　　　*Synonym:*

4. theme

Guess:　　　　　　　*Word Meaning:*　　　　　　*Synonym:*

Continued →

Exercise 3 (Continued)

5. precipitate

    Guess: *Word Meaning:*   *Synonym:*

6. infraction

    Guess: *Word Meaning:*   *Synonym:*

7. covert

    Guess: *Word Meaning:*   *Synonym:*

8. gratuitous

    Guess: *Word Meaning:*   *Synonym:*

9. procrastinate

    Guess: *Word Meaning:*   *Synonym:*

10. reconcile

    Guess: *Word Meaning:*   *Synonym:*

11. provocative

    Guess: *Word Meaning:*   *Synonym:*

12. stimulating

    Guess: *Word Meaning:*   *Synonym:*

13. diverse

    Guess: *Word Meaning:*   *Synonym:*

14. indifferent

    Guess: *Word Meaning:*   *Synonym:*

15. extraterrestrial

    Guess: *Word Meaning:*   *Synonym:*

16. corroborate

    Guess: *Word Meaning:*   *Synonym:*

17. perceptive

    Guess: *Word Meaning:*   *Synonym:*

Continued →

Exercise 3 (Continued)

18. absolve

   Guess: *Word Meaning:*   *Synonym:*

19. enhance

   Guess: *Word Meaning:*   *Synonym:*

20. antidote

   Guess: *Word Meaning:*   *Synonym:*

21. redundant

   Guess: *Word Meaning:*   *Synonym:*

22. commonplace

   Guess: *Word Meaning:*   *Synonym:*

23. adjoining

   Guess: *Word Meaning:*   *Synonym:*

24. aggravate

   Guess: *Word Meaning:*   *Synonym:*

25. paraphrase

   Guess: *Word Meaning:*   *Synonym:*

26. indecision

   Guess: *Word Meaning:*   *Synonym:*

EXERCISE 4

Match the vocabulary word with its synonym.

Test Tip   *A synonym is a word that has the same or nearly the same meaning.*

    1. _____   malediction   A. shorten

    2. _____   unwieldy   B. temporary

    3. _____   divulge   C. messy

Continued ➡

Exercise 4 (Continued)

4. _____	unkempt	D. beginner
5. _____	transient	E. surface
6. _____	curtail	F. steal
7. _____	congenial	G. bulky
8. _____	superficial	H. curse
9. _____	embezzle	I. friendly
10. _____	novice	J. reveal
11. _____	saga	K. unaware
12. _____	wary	L. rigid
13. _____	oblivious	M. story
14. _____	taut	N. unreasonable
15. _____	persevere	O. suspicious
16. _____	chaos	P. destroy
17. _____	eradicate	Q. confusion
18. _____	laudatory	R. continue
19. _____	irrational	S. praised
20. _____	adequate	T. first
21. _____	original	U. move back
22. _____	transparent	V. picture
23. _____	recede	W. hesitant
24. _____	reluctant	X. see through
25. _____	image	Y. enough

EXERCISE 5

Match the vocabulary word with its synonym.

1. _____	alleviate	A. diseased
2. _____	antiseptic	B. rid
3. _____	pathology	C. cleanse
4. _____	purify	D. difference
5. _____	recuperate	E. sterile

Continued →

Exercise 5 (Continued)

6. _____	unresponsive	F.	renew
7. _____	secrete	G.	regret
8. _____	discrepancy	H.	puzzling
9. _____	indistinct	I.	unclear
10. _____	unyielding	J.	ooze
11. _____	quizzical	K.	firm
12. _____	immaculate	L.	confirm
13. _____	verify	M.	recover
14. _____	devious	N.	routine
15. _____	timorous	O.	suspicious
16. _____	contrition	P.	cruel
17. _____	expedite	Q.	reject
18. _____	indistinct	R.	hurry up
19. _____	disrupting	S.	obvious
20. _____	renovate	T.	shy
21. _____	diligent	U.	unspoiled
22. _____	blatant	V.	scold
23. _____	repudiate	W.	upset
24. _____	berate	X.	hardworking
25. _____	sadistic	Y.	motionless

EXERCISE 6

Match the vocabulary word with its synonym.

1. _____	crass	A.	character
2. _____	vulnerable	B.	shocking
3. _____	dispassionate	C.	rival
4. _____	slovenly	D.	nauseated
5. _____	indigenous	E.	type
6. _____	minuscule	F.	grumbler

Continued →

Exercise 6 (Continued)

7. _____	therapeutic	G.	typical
8. _____	symptomatic	H.	sympathy
9. _____	genre	I.	return
10. _____	persona	J.	beneficial
11. _____	traumatic	K.	showy
12. _____	nemesis	L.	undetectable
13. _____	queasy	M.	tiny
14. _____	empathy	N.	pattern
15. _____	malcontent	O.	dull
16. _____	remand	P.	unfeeling
17. _____	syndrome	Q.	praise
18. _____	lackluster	R.	moist
19. _____	kudos	S.	foul
20. _____	dank	T.	trainee
21. _____	fetid	U.	dirty
22. _____	protégé	V.	bond
23. _____	flamboyant	W.	hesitant
24. _____	imperceptible	X.	calm
25. _____	rapport	Y.	native

EXERCISE 7

Circle the word that does **not** belong in each word group.

1. Unite   disjoin   fuse   coalesce
2. Calm   composure   impatience   equanimity
3. Adulation   protection   hostility   patronage
4. Pretentious   proud   pleasant   self-respecting
5. Dissension   argument   fighting   agreement
6. Grandiose   modest   super   extraordinary
7. Slovenly   well-groomed   attractive   clean
8. Beneficial   humanitarian   harmful   constructive
9. Remorseful   boastful   sorry   penitent
10. Permanent   fleeting   long-lived   never-ending

Continued →

Exercise 7 (Continued)

11. Weary	exhausted	energetic	languid
12. Fugitive	escapee	prisoner	derelict
13. Explosive	peaceful	eruptive	volatile
14. Pilfer	take	embezzle	return
15. Present	truant	AWOL	missing

EXERCISE 8

Circle the word that does **not** belong in each word group.

1. Tardy	belated	timely	overdue
2. Trim	shorten	reduce	lengthen
3. Confess	hide	reveal	divulge
4. Abbreviate	shorten	extend	prove
5. Harmful	beneficial	deleterious	grisly
6. Avarice	greed	generosity	excess
7. Corroborate	report	confirm	refute
8. Covert	secret	public	undercover
9. Coalition	union	alliance	outsider
10. Inadvertent	accidental	intentional	unconsidered
11. Verbose	wordy	brief	loquacious
12. Unfounded	supported	substantiated	demonstrable
13. Introduction	prologue	epilogue	preamble
14. Condensed	short	concise	expanded
15. Cursory	shallow	superficial	complete

EXERCISE 9

Circle the word that does **not** belong in each word group.

1. Unappealing	pleasant	tasteful	lovely
2. Invention	innovation	choreography	improvisation
3. Master	maestro	novice	expert
4. New	contemporary	up-to-date	antique
5. Immaculate	fallible	flawless	impeccable

Continued →

Exercise 9 (Continued)

6. Regret   remorse   pride   contrition
7. Confirm   question   validate   verify
8. Critic   detractor   advocate   censor
9. Sterile   fertile   prolific   fruitful
10. Rationale   guess   reason   thinking

EXERCISE 4 ANSWERS

1. H	10. D	19. N
2. G	11. M	20. Y
3. J	12. O	21. T
4. C	13. K	22. X
5. B	14. L	23. U
6. A	15. R	24. W
7. I	16. Q	25. V
8. E	17. P	
9. F	18. S	

EXERCISE 5 ANSWERS

1. B	10. K	19. W
2. E	11. H	20. F
3. A	12. U	21. X
4. C	13. L	22. S
5. M	14. O	23. Q
6. Y	15. T	24. V
7. J	16. G	25. P
8. D	17. R	
9. N	18. I	

EXERCISE 6 ANSWERS

1. P	6. M	11. B
2. S	7. J	12. C
3. X	8. G	13. D
4. U	9. E	14. H
5. Y	10. A	15. F

16. I	20. R	24. L
17. N	21. S	25. V
18. O	22. T	
19. Q	23. K	

EXERCISE 7 ANSWERS

1. disjoin	6. modest	11. energetic
2. impatience	7. slovenly	12. prisoner
3. hostility	8. harmful	13. peaceful
4. pretentious	9. boastful	14. return
5. agreement	10. fleeting	15. present

EXERCISE 8 ANSWERS

1. timely	6. generosity	11. brief
2. lengthen	7. refute	12. unfounded
3. hide	8. public	13. epilogue
4. extend	9. outsider	14. expanded
5. beneficial	10. intentional	15. complete

EXERCISE 9 ANSWERS

1. unappealing	5. fallible	9. sterile
2. choreography	6. pride	10. guess
3. novice	7. question	
4. antique	8. advocate	

SOUND OFF WITH YOUR WORD KNOWLEDGE

You know that there are many ways to expand your vocabulary. Not all of them will be equally effective in preparing for the AFQT. The key to vocabulary building is to work *strategically*. We've said this many times in this chapter because it's so important: You'll never know every word in the English language, but if you can get a good understanding of word roots, prefixes, and suffixes, you'll be in a much better position to answer the Word Knowledge questions correctly.

SO, WHAT'S THE PLAN?

Now that you've got the tools, let's see how well you use them. The Word Knowledge section of the AFQT includes both synonyms and words in context. Take the following Word Knowledge Practice Test under real test conditions; that is to say, allow 11 minutes to complete the 35 questions.

> *Make learning new words a game. When you learn a new word, use it often in one day in different ways. You might annoy your friends, but you'll have fun learning!*

You can now begin the test.

Practice Set: Word Knowledge

This is a test of your knowledge of word meanings. These questions consist of a sentence or phrase with a word or phrase that is underlined. From the answer choices given, decide which choice means the same or most nearly the same as the underlined word or phrase.

1. Notorious most nearly means
   A. unconcerned.
   B. famous.
   C. drab.
   D. generous.

2. My high school biology teacher loved to _____ from science topics into personal stories about his own high school days.
   A. distract
   B. digress
   C. discredit
   D. divulge

3. Agile most nearly means
   A. graceful.
   B. disturbed.
   C. sudden.
   D. adept.

4. Despite their past disagreements, the members of the squad were able to form an amicable working relationship.
   A. intelligent
   B. brief
   C. agreeable
   D. weak

5. The major decided to <u>refurbish</u> the house himself so he could finally sell it.

   A. rebuild

   B. demolish

   C. depress

   D. ignite

6. The politician's <u>superficial</u> smile was a clue that she might not be sincere.

   A. convincing

   B. wise

   C. showy

   D. phony

7. <u>Divisive</u> means

   A. disruptive.

   B. superior.

   C. appropriate.

   D. clumsy.

8. <u>Antagonist</u> most nearly means

   A. stranger.

   B. friend.

   C. colleague.

   D. opponent.

9. The private was given an <u>erroneous</u> message to report to the conference room.

   A. false

   B. appropriate

   C. classified

   D. planned

10. <u>Apathy</u> most nearly means
    A. passion.
    B. indifference.
    C. laziness.
    D. goodness.

11. <u>Terse</u> most nearly means
    A. concise.
    B. wordy.
    C. extraordinary.
    D. related.

12. She received the highest honor for <u>meritorious</u> service.
    A. unremarkable
    B. praiseworthy
    C. proper
    D. genuine

13. <u>Delve</u> most nearly means
    A. climb.
    B. explore.
    C. believe.
    D. accept.

14. <u>Accessible</u> most nearly means
    A. available.
    B. aloof.
    C. belittled.
    D. ashen.

15. <u>Coddle</u> most nearly means
    A. pamper.
    B. denounce.
    C. deter.
    D. honor.

16. <u>Illicit</u> most nearly means
    A. humane.
    B. concise.
    C. improper.
    D. stormy.

17. Thomas was fired for foolishly <u>divulging</u> company secrets on Facebook.
    A. dangling.
    B. predicting.
    C. disclosing.
    D. removing.

18. <u>Prolific</u> most nearly means
    A. sterile.
    B. fruitful.
    C. wasteful.
    D. brief.

19. <u>Inaccurate</u> most nearly means
    A. concise.
    B. appropriate.
    C. incorrrect.
    D. revealing.

20. The sergeant seemed, to many unhappy recruits, to give <u>irrational</u> orders.

    A. understandable

    B. questionable

    C. reserved

    D. clear

21. Some companies replace <u>obsolete</u> machinery to keep current.

    A. out-of-date

    B. unbelievable

    C. unremarkable

    D. unique

22. <u>Ironic</u> most nearly means

    A. convenient.

    B. sarcastic.

    C. poor.

    D. unaware.

23. <u>Demise</u> most nearly means

    A. death.

    B. duration.

    C. rebirth.

    D. late.

24. <u>Pliable</u> most nearly means

    A. pompous.

    B. genial.

    C. incoherent.

    D. flexible.

25. Verbatim most nearly means
    A. emotional.
    B. exact.
    C. definite.
    D. rigid.

26. Irate most nearly means
    A. rash.
    B. enraged.
    C. hasty.
    D. cordial.

27. A cup of tepid coffee will definitely not warm you up on a cold morning.
    A. hot
    B. scalding
    C. decaffeinated
    D. lukewarm

28. Placid most nearly means
    A. stormy.
    B. calm.
    C. difficult.
    D. silent.

29. The mythological beast unleashed his wrath on the frightened citizens.
    A. fury
    B. sting
    C. exuberance
    D. timidity

30. <u>Sedate</u> most nearly means
    A. flashy.
    B. harmful.
    C. quiet.
    D. heartless.

31. <u>Temporary</u> most nearly means
    A. short.
    B. drowsy.
    C. eager.
    D. devoted.

32. The soldier's disregard for his orders put everyone in <u>jeopardy</u>.
    A. danger
    B. guilt
    C. security
    D. punishment

33. <u>Hypothesize</u> most nearly means
    A. deny.
    B. help.
    C. deliver.
    D. suppose.

34. <u>Dank</u> most nearly means
    A. moist and humid.
    B. sunny and warm.
    C. cloudy and cold.
    D. hot and rainy.

35. <u>Accolade</u> most nearly means
    A. peace.
    B. award.
    C. truth.
    D. trickery.

ANSWERS AND EXPLANATIONS

1. The correct answer is (B), *famous*, which means "generally known or famous for." *Unconcerned*, choice (A), means "uninterested." *Drab*, choice (C), means "dull," and *generous*, choice (D), means "liberal in giving" or "unselfish."

2. The correct answer is (B), *digress*. The teacher may have intended to *distract*, choice (A), his students from what they should be learning, but the sentence doesn't support that. *Discredit*, choice (C), means "to demean or disgrace" and *divulge*, choice (A), means "to tell."

3. The correct answer is (A). *Agile* means having a ready ability to move with quick, easy grace and to be "nimble and well-coordinated." *Disturbed* (choice B) means "showing symptoms of emotional illness." While choice C, *sudden*, can mean "quick," it clearly is not synonymous with *agile*. To be *adept* (choice D) is to be "skillful."

4. The correct answer is (C), *agreeable*. *Amicable* means "friendly goodwill, sociable." *Intelligent* (choice A) means "very smart," *brief* (choice B) means "short, as in time," and *weak* (choice D) means "lacking strength."

5. The correct answer is (A). To *refurbish* is "to renovate or to rebuild." *Demolish* (choice B) means "to destroy or tear down," which is the opposite of the concept "to rebuild." Choice C (*depress*) makes no sense since it means "to press down." To *ignite* (D) means "to set fire to." Obviously, if the major sets fire to the house, he can't sell it!

6. The correct answer is choice (D), *phony.* The clue to figuring out the correct answer is in the words "might not be sincere." Someone who is insincere can be "phony." *Convincing* (A) means "persuading by argument or evidence." A smile is not usually described as "wise" (B), although the person who is smiling could be wise and that wise person could be *showy* (C), which means "gaudy or loud."

7. The correct answer is *disruptive* (A), which means "to cause disagreement or to force a separation." *Superior* (B) is "higher in rank or importance," *appropriate* (C) means "suitable or fitting in," and *clumsy* means "to be awkward" or "without skill or grace."

8. The correct answer is (D), *opponent.* An *antagonist* is a person who is "opposed to, struggles against, or competes with another person." The person can be a stranger, a colleague, even someone you thought was your friend, but by definition, choices A, B, and C are incorrect answer choices.

9. The correct answer is (A). *Erroneous* means "incorrect." While it may have been *appropriate* (B) to hand over a *false* (A) message, perhaps because the true message was *classified* (C), which means "confidential," *erroneous* most nearly means "false." *Planned* (D) is incorrect.

10. The correct answer is (B). *Apathy* means "not caring." *Passion* (A) is the opposite of *apathy,* while *laziness* (C) means "not willing to work." *Goodness* (D) means "the state or quality of being good."

11. The correct answer is (A), *concise. Terse* means "brief to the point of being rude." *Wordy* (B) is an opposite concept. *Extraordinary* (C) means "so unusual as to be remarkable." *Related* (D) means "to show or to have connection to."

12. The correct answer is *praiseworthy* (B). *Meritorious* means "deserving praise, reward." *Unremarkable* (A) and *genuine* (D) "service" would not seem to be deserving of an award. *Proper* (C) means "right."

13. The correct answer is *explore* (B). (A), *climb* is "to move up." To *believe* (C) is to "trust." *Accept* (D) is to "take."

14. The correct answer is (A), *available. Aloof* (B) means to be "standoffish or unfriendly." (C), *belittled,* is "to regard something or someone as less than important" and (D), *ashen,* means "extremely pale or drained of color."

15. The correct answer is (A), *pamper. Coddle* means "to treat tenderly." *Denounce* (B) means "to condemn," while *honor* (D) means "to hold in respect or esteem."

16. The correct answer is (C), *improper.* To be *humane* (A) is to "be tender, compassionate, sympathetic towards people and animals." *Concise* (B) means "to the point" and *stormy* (D) is "affected by storms" or " a violent action, sometimes a violent speech."

17. The correct answer is (C), *disclosing,* which means "revealing or disclosing something private or secret." *Dangling* (A) is "holding something that is swaying." *Predicting* means "telling in advance or foretelling." *Removing* (D) is "taking something away."

18. The correct answer is (B), *fruitful.* It means "to be extremely productive." *Sterile* (A) is "free from any germs" and can also mean "barren or not productive." *Wasteful* (C) is "extremely extravagant" and *brief* (D) means "short" or even "abrupt."

19. *Inaccurate* most nearly means (C), " incorrect or erroneous." Choice (A), *concise* means, "brief but comprehensive." Another word for *concise* is *pithy. Appropriate* (B) means "suitable for the occasion," while (D), *revealing,* means "exposing part of the body that would normally be kept covered" or "giving away information."

20. The correct answer is (B), *questionable. Irrational* means " lacking in reason." *Understandable* (A) and *clear* (D) are opposite in meaning. *Reserved,* choice (C), means "composed."

21. The correct answer is *out-of-date* (A) or "no longer usable." *Unbelievable* (B), if you remember the meaning of the prefix "-un," means "not believable." *Unremarkable* (C) and *unique* are opposites, meaning "ordinary" and "different," respectively.

22. The correct answer is (B), *sarcastic* or "words to suggest the opposite of what the speaker really means." *Convenient* (A) means "useful or suitable," *poor* (C) means "without funds or money," and *unaware* (D) means "not aware" or "not conscious of something."

23. The correct answer is *death* (A). *Duration* (B) is "length of time." *Rebirth* (C) is "the revival of something that was destroyed". *Late* (D) is "not on time."

24. The correct answer is *flexible* (D) or "easily bent." It can also mean "easily influenced." *Pompous* (A) is "arrogant." *Genial* (B) is "friendly or gracious" and *incoherent* (C) is "unable to be understood."

25. The correct answer is *exact* (B) or "word for word." *Emotional* (A) means "expressing strong feelings or emotions." *Definite* (C) is "fixed or rigid," and *rigid* (D) means "unbending" or "not flexible."

26. The correct answer is *enraged* (B). *Rash* (A) is "an ill-conceived haste" or "acting quickly before thinking." *Hasty* (C) is "very quickly" and *cordial* means "in a friendly manner."

27. The correct answer is *lukewarm* (D) or "slightly warm." *Hot* (A) and *scalding* (B) are much hotter than "lukewarm." *Decaffeinated* (C) is "without caffeine."

28. The correct answer is *calm,* (B). *Placid* is "pleasantly calm" or "tranquil." *Stormy* (A) is certainly not "calm or tranquil," stormy means "a violent commotion." *Difficult* (C) is "hard" and *silent* means "without sound."

29. The correct answer is *fury* (A) or "violent anger." *Sting* (B) is "a sharp mental or physical pain" and in the context of the sentence, one would expect a "beast" to unleash more than a "sting" on frightened citizens. *Exuberance* (C) is "a state of wild joy and *enthusiasm* and *timidity* (D) is "a state of fear."

30. The correct answer is *quiet* (C). *Flashy* (A) is "showy or gaudy," *harmful* (B) is "to cause harm," and *heartless* (D) means "unfeeling or cruel."

31. The correct answer is *short* (A) or "not permanent." *Drowsy* (B) is "sleepy," *eager* (C) means "to be impatient," and *devoted* (D) means "loyal."

32. The correct answer is *danger* (A) or "risk." *Guilt* (B) means "to feel remorse for some crime or offense" and *security* (C) means "to be free from danger." *Punishment* (D) is "a penalty for an offense or crime."

33. The correct answer is *suppose* (D), or more accurately, "to speculate." *Deny* (A) means "to withhold." *Help* (B) means to "make easier" or "contribute to." *Deliver* (C) means " to give to someone."

34. The correct answer is (A), "moist and humid." "Sunny and warm"(B) is positive, "cloudy and cold" is the opposite. "Hot and rainy" isn't specific enough.

35. The correct answer is *award* (B). Accolades are awards and honors presented. *Peace* (A) and *truth* (C) are positive terms, but do not mean an award, and *trickery* (D) has no connection to *accolade*.

Paragraph Comprehension

WHAT TO EXPECT IN THE PARAGRAPH COMPREHENSION SECTION OF THE AFQT

You know that the Paragraph Comprehension section is designed to measure your reading comprehension skills. It is composed of reading passages followed by questions. The passages are brief and the questions are in multiple-choice format. Everything you need to answer the questions correctly can be found in the passage. In other words, the questions in this section do not ask you anything that requires any outside knowledge. But you do have to know how to find the information you need quickly.

Test Tip

You don't have to know anything about the topic of the passage to answer the questions.

ACTIVITIES TO INCREASE YOUR READING COMPREHENSION

1. Read books, newspapers (in print and/or online), magazines (in print and/or online), and anything else made up of words.

   Anything you read makes you a better reader. Read whatever you want, but try sometimes to read something of substance. That is science, current events, social studies, history . . . you understand. The newspaper is a wonderful source that provides text in different formats, covering different topics and opinions. Try this: read an article from each newspaper section every day for new information and as a way to practice reading different types of content. For example, the front page of the newspaper will expose you to "informational" news, the editorial page will expose you to opinions, and the arts section will expose you to criticism.

2. As you read, stop when you come across any unknown words and look them up.

   If you read online, it's easy to open an online dictionary and type in the word. But, if you don't want to stop every time you encounter an unfamiliar word, try to figure out the meaning of the word in the context of the sentence. Later you can find out if your definition was correct. If you remember, in Chapter 2 we recommended this process for answering Word Knowledge questions.

3. Learn words by studying words.

   The better and bigger your vocabulary, the easier it is to understand what you're reading. In the previous chapter (Chapter 2), you learned how to improve your vocabulary. This will also help you on the Paragraph Comprehension section of the AFQT. Study word parts. Knowing the root words will help you recognize word parts in other words you'll encounter in the passages.

4. Did we say, "Read (it's important)"?

   You'll begin to increase your vocabulary just by reading. The more you read, the greater your chances of coming across unknown words. Even if you have seen the word only once, it's better than not at all. After all, you might remember something from that first time that triggers a clue to help you answer a question correctly when you see the word again on the test.

> *When you see a word you don't know, try to determine the meaning from the words and sentences around that unfamiliar word. If that doesn't work, try to ignore the word and focus on the overall meaning of the paragraph or passage.*

TYPES OF PARAGRAPH COMPREHENSION QUESTIONS

There are six types of Paragraph Comprehension questions on the AFQT:

- Words in context—define a vocabulary word from the passage.

- Main idea—identify the main idea of the passage, choose the best title for the passage, or identify the primary theme of the passage.

- Specific details—identify a specific fact or detail in the passage.

- Author's purpose—determine why the author wrote the passage.

- Author's tone—determine how the author feels about the subject of the passage.

- Inference—interpreting something you read, analyze the author's meaning, and make an inference based on the passage.

WORDS IN CONTEXT

Since you won't have access to a dictionary or thesaurus while taking the ASVAB, you have to use context clues to figure out the meaning of an unknown word. These words-in-context questions ask you to recognize the meaning of a word as it is used in a sentence in the paragraph. There are different types of context clues, and knowing what to look for will help you with the "words in context" question types.

SAMPLE PASSAGE:

There are lots of big, obvious ways to become a better bicycle rider. Learn how to lift the rear or figure out that shifting thing. There are also a few small but important techniques. They aren't flashy, and chances are, none of your friends (except the most skilled) will recognize that you have them. But these things will make a huge difference in how you ride. One of the coolest techniques is learning how to spin the pedals. Mountain bikers tend to be <u>mashers</u>. They chop the pedals, pushing down with hard, heavy leg motions. This style looks impressive, but it robs power, because energy is being transmitted through less than half of the pedal stroke. The idea is to deliver energy throughout as much of the pedal stroke as possible. Pedaling in smooth circles raises your speed, increases traction, uses less energy, and even improves your balance and handling. Some people like to make a big deal out of finding the optimum cadence—at least 90 revolutions per minute (rpm) on flat roads.

1. In this paragraph, the word <u>mashers</u> most nearly means cyclists who

   A. push down on the pedals.

   B. ride fast.

   C. win races.

   D. are flashy riders.

The meaning of "mashers" is obvious because the sentence that follows actually defines the term: "They chop the pedals pushing down with hard, heavy leg motions." This is probably the easiest type of vocabulary-in-context question.

More than likely, the majority of the vocabulary-in-context questions will look more like this:

2. The word <u>cadence</u> means

    A. end of a phrase.

    B. speed of pedaling.

    C. gear shifting.

    D. measure of rhythm.

In this passage, "cadence" means how fast the cyclist is pedaling. The sentence that follows provides you with the clues you need: "at least 90 revolutions per minute." "Cadence" also means the measure of a rhythm in a musical verse or phrase or the close of a musical phrase. However, the paragraph is not about music; it's about bicycle riding.

To correctly answer vocabulary-in-context questions,

- Read a sentence or two before and after the word being tested.

- Come up with a word that could replace the word.

- Get rid of answer choices that don't fit.

- To test the remaining answer choices, read them back into the sentence in place of the original word.

- Always beware of the synonyms of the word that don't match the word's meaning in the paragraph.

Test Tip   *Some words have more than one definition. Be ready.*

MAIN IDEA

Main idea questions ask about the meaning of the paragraph as a whole. It is the most important "idea." To find the main idea means you have to get through all of the paragraph's details to find the most important one. The main idea can be the general idea with less important details that support it.

Example:

Which of the following would most likely be the main idea of the sample paragraph above?

   A. All cyclists ride in the same manner.

   B. Learning to spin the pedals can make you a more efficient rider.

   C. There is only one way to ride efficiently.

   D. Anyone can learn to ride a bicycle.

The passage is primarily concerned with teaching the technique that will result in a more efficient ride: pedaling in smooth circles. The main idea is actually stated in the following sentence: "One of the coolest techniques is learning how to spin the pedals."

To correctly answer main-idea questions:

• Read the whole passage/paragraph before you answer the question.

• Try to answer without re-reading the passage.

• Be careful of words like *all*, *always*, *never*, and *must*.

The main idea *sums up* the paragraph and the other sentences in the passage support or back up the main idea. The other sentences that surround the main idea may give details that further explain the main idea. Those details and facts are the clues that will lead you to the main idea. Sometimes the main idea is somewhere in the first couple of sentences. In the paragraph above, that's not the case.

Test Tip   *Main-idea questions ask about the passage as a whole.*

Another type of main-idea question will ask you to choose the best title for the passage or paragraph. The best title best expresses the main idea.

Example:

Based on the sample paragraph above, which would be the best title?

> **A.** Becoming a Flashy Mountain Cyclist
>
> **B.** All You Need Is Speed
>
> **C.** Perfect Your Pedaling Technique
>
> **D.** What Is Cadence?

The best title is (C). It describes the paragraph as a whole and is supported by specific details. Or, you could think about it this way: "What would be the one sentence that could sum up the whole paragraph?" The whole point of the paragraph is to support the main idea!

DETAIL QUESTIONS

Detail questions may ask you to describe setting and characters, while others ask you to determine their importance. All detail questions ask you to identify a specific "detail" or piece of information that's found in the passage. This is probably the easiest of the paragraph comprehension question types.

To correctly answer a detail question,

- First, read the question before you read the passage.

- Skim the passage to find the sentence or sentences that contain the correct answer.

- Then read a sentence that contains the information about a specific detail carefully.

Test Tip

Some answers may look right because they relate to the passage. But remember, the correct answer has to be in the passage.

Example:

In the sample paragraph above, what happens when mountain cyclists "mash" the pedals?

    A. Mashing causes the cyclist to lose power.

    B. They become better riders.

    C. They increase the tire traction.

    D. Mashing makes little difference in how the cyclist rides.

The answer to this detail question is (A). You can find the answer in the sentence, "This style looks impressive, but it robs power, because energy is being transmitted through less than half of the pedal stroke."

AUTHOR'S PURPOSE (OR, WHY DID THE AUTHOR WRITE THIS PASSAGE?)

This question type involves asking you to figure out why the author wrote what she or he wrote. The author's purpose often comes in these varieties:

- To describe,
- persuade,
- teach or inform,
- compare and/or contrast,
- direct, or
- entertain.

Example:

In the sample paragraph above, what is the author's purpose?

    A. To entertain cyclists

    B. To compare road cyclists to mountain bikers

    C. To inform bikers on effective techniques

    D. To prove a point

The correct answer is (C). The purpose of the passage is to teach (inform) mountain bikers about the most effective pedaling techniques. The passage does not try to entertain and does not try to prove a point. It mentions ineffective cycling techniques but does not make any comparisons.

AUTHOR'S TONE

Another type of question that requires you to "get into the head of the author" is the question that asks you to identify the author's attitude or tone. The tone is how the author's feelings are presented in the passage or paragraph. The tone can be formal, informal, serious, or humorous. It can also be positive, negative, or impartial. The author's tone shows an author's attitude toward the subject. It can simply be informative or neutral if the passage attempts to instruct. You can't actually hear the author reading the paragraph; all you can do is to read carefully.

 **Test Tip**

Don't get caught up with the details. The answers to all of the questions for a paragraph are guaranteed to be in the paragraph! You don't have to understand the paragraph completely.

Example:

In the sample paragraph above, what is the author's tone?

    A. Humorous

    B. Somber

    C. Informal

    D. Formal

The author presents the information in an informal manner. It seems as though the author is teaching the reader in an informal and sometimes entertaining way. Some of the paragraph may be humorous, but the tone of the entire paragraph is more informal. The writing style is certainly neither somber nor formal.

If the question of tone is about the paragraph as a whole, try to keep in mind what the author wrote that gave you the best impression of how she or he feels about the topic.

INFERENCE

Inference questions ask you to read between the lines. To answer these questions, you have to figure out (again) what the author thinks or means, but doesn't directly say. Inference questions will look like this:

The author suggests that . . .

The passage suggests that . . .

The author implies that . . .

What does the passage imply about . . .

What can be inferred about . . .

To correctly answer inference questions,

- Reread the relevant information in the paragraph.

- Focus your attention on what the question means in the context of the paragraph.

- There must be evidence to support your answer choice.

Example:

The sample paragraph above implies which of the following about the decrease in energy use if you pedal in smooth circles?

     A. You can ride longer.

     B. You can lift the wheel easier.

     C. You will decrease traction.

     D. You will decrease power output.

The correct answer is (A). The idea is to deliver energy throughout as much of the pedal stroke as possible. If you use less energy this way, it stands to reason that you can ride longer.

STRATEGIES TO MAKE YOU A MORE ACTIVE READER

To understand a passage, you have to be able to identify the main idea and the author's purpose and to follow the author's reasoning. You have to know how to "interact" with the words as you read them. To hone your active reading skills before you take the test, you should

1. Mark up the text you are reading. Circling and underlining important words and phrases will
   - help you find the ideas and information you need to understand what you're reading,
   - give you an opportunity to review and recap the text.

     Circle or underline key words or phrases that help you remember the idea or point that's made in the sentence or that part of the text. Mark up the keywords that connect the ideas in the text. Use arrows to connect the words that make clear the main idea statement(s), major supporting details, and points that suggest the author's tone and purpose.

2. Take notes in the margins.
   - Make notes to summarize paragraphs.
   - If the text includes names you may need to know, note them by linking them.
   - Make observations about the overall structure of the text. Perhaps the text compares or contrasts ideas.
   - Understanding how the text is organized will help you recognize the text's main idea and main purpose and distinguish details from the main idea.

3. Don't get distracted by minor details as you read. If you try to remember all of the details as you read, you'll never find the main idea and you'll get bogged down. In the margins of the

text you're reading, make notes of where particular examples are located. (Of course, don't do any of these things if you're reading a library book!)

4. **Sum up the text after you read it.** Take a couple minutes to summarize what you've read. What was the main idea and what were the important supporting details?

When you work on the paragraphs in the following Practice Test, jot down quick summaries of the paragraph while you're reading it. After you finish reading *this* book, read lots of anything else—books, newspapers, magazines, novels, biographies, even poetry. A great way to practice your reading comprehension skills is to join a book club. In a book club, you get the opportunity to discuss your ideas about what you're reading in a group.

SO, WHAT'S THE PLAN?

Now that you've got the tools, let's see how well you use them. The Paragraph Comprehension section of the AFQT includes 15 questions based on several short passages written on a variety of topics. Take the following Paragraph Comprehension Practice Test yourself under real test conditions, that is, allow 13 minutes to complete the 15 questions.

Test Tip

Detail questions may contain wrong answers that are tempting. Those "tempting" wrong answer choices usually misuse the details from the passage.

You can now begin the test.

Practice Set: Paragraph Comprehension

This is a test of your ability to understand what you read. In this section you will find one or more paragraphs of reading material followed by statements or questions. Read each paragraph and select the answer choice that best completes the statement or answers the question.

PASSAGE 1

Absentees and managers have very different perspectives on why people miss work. The usual excuse is illness. In reality, we don't know how much absence is due to legitimate illness. When people are asked in confidence why they are typically absent from work, they usually mention some common medical problem, but there is often reason to doubt them. People tend to explain behavior that may be viewed negatively by others, like absenteeism, in terms of factors beyond their control. Because being sick is accepted by our culture as a legitimate reason that is beyond a person's control, it's reasonable for people to explain their absences in medical terms. While people normally explain their absences in terms of sickness, managers and other employees often have less forgiving explanations: laziness, irresponsibility, or a poor work ethic. Since most people don't miss much work, the person who is frequently absent is often described in negative terms.

1. The main purpose of the passage is to
   A. analyze why most workers miss work.
   B. describe the attitudes toward absenteeism.
   C. suggest how to keep workers in the workplace.
   D. provide workers with excuses.

2. It can be inferred from the passage that

   A. people are often ashamed to admit to minor illnesses.

   B. people never miss work for non-medical reasons.

   C. managers are always concerned about unexplained absences.

   D. workers are often concerned about what the other workers think of them.

3. As used in the passage, the word *legitimate* (line 3) most nearly means

   A. lawful.

   B. unwarranted.

   C. accepted.

   D. unjust.

PASSAGE 2

Music's power to affect moods and stir emotions has been well known for as long as music has existed. The healing power of music, taken for granted by ancient cultures, is only recently becoming accepted by medical professionals as a way of healing the emotionally ill. Using musical activities involving patients, the music therapist seeks to restore mental and physical health. Music therapists usually work with emotionally disturbed patients as part of a team of therapists and doctors. Music therapists work together with physicians, psychiatrists, psychologists, physical therapists, nurses, teachers, recreation leaders, and families of patients. Hospitals, schools, retirement homes, and community agencies and clinics are some of the sites where music therapists work.

4. What is the main idea of the passage?

   A. Not only can music entertain, it can also heal.

   B. Music therapy is not accepted by medical professionals.

   C. Music therapists must participate in training internships.

   D. Music therapy can be done anywhere.

5. You can infer that a following paragraph would most likely discuss which of the following?

   A. Which doctors are part of the therapy process

   B. What music therapy actually is

   C. Where music therapists typically work

   D. Which professionals do not accept music therapy as valid

PASSAGE 3

Puerto Rico is unique among Caribbean destinations because of the shear breadth of experiences available to you. If you crave a luxury resort, you'll find several world-class options to choose from. If you're a nature lover, you'll find an abundance of wonders to explore. If you're a surfer or an art aficionado, a golfer or history buff, a deep-sea diver, or a gourmet, you'll find satisfaction here. And perhaps foremost, lending a distinctive flavor to any Puerto Rico experience, you'll find a sophisticated, centuries-old culture—a mix of Native American, Spanish, African, and contemporary United States influences.

6. All of the following activities are mentioned EXCEPT

   A. surfing.

   B. golfing.

   C. diving.

   D. horseback riding.

7. The word *shear* most likely means

   A. shorten.

   B. reduce.

   C. highest.

   D. curtailed.

PASSAGE 4

Advocates of hybrid vehicles believe that they offer the best short-term solution to some long-term problems. By combining a regular gasoline-powered engine with an electric engine, hybrids cut down on gas consumption and decrease the pollution caused by gasoline engines. These cars help auto makers meet government regulations for fuel efficiency and emissions controls. Some auto makers do not think that hybrids are the answer for the future, but these small cars provide a way for conservation-conscious consumers to do something for the environment. Other auto makers see another benefit to the development process for hybrids. The technology that has gone into creating and refining the dual-powered hybrid will help with the longer-term development of cars powered by hydrogen fuel cells.

8. According to the passage, hybrids are beneficial for all of the following reasons EXCEPT they

   A. decrease gas use.

   B. provide information for developing hydrogen fuel cells.

   C. decrease pollution.

   D. provide a new way for auto makers to make more money.

9. The tone of the passage is

   A. entertaining.

   B. humorous.

   C. informative.

   D. somber.

PASSAGE 5

In his first year in office, President Bill Clinton attempted to lift the ban on gays in the military. Instead, Congress fashioned the Military Personnel Eligibility Act of 1993, otherwise known as "Don't Ask, Don't Tell (DADT)." The compromise allowed gays to serve as long as they kept their sexual orientation quiet, and prohibited superiors from asking about it. Since 1993, more than 13,500 service members have been discharged for being gay. In the fall of 2010, a California district judge ruled DADT unconstitutional and ordered an immediate stop to its enforcement. In the winter of 2010, the House and Senate voted on and repealed DADT. On December 22, President Barack Obama signed the policy into law. DADT remains in effect, however, until the Pentagon certifies the military's readiness on such issues as benefits for gay military families.

10. What is the author's position on the Military Personnel Eligibility Act of 1993?

A. Neutral

B. Conflicted

C. Positive

D. Negative

11. The passage states which one of the following was president of the United States when the "Don't Ask, Don't Tell" law went into effect?

A. George H. W. Bush

B. George W. Bush

C. Bill Clinton

D. Barack Obama

12. According to the passage, which of the following is TRUE?

A. The repeal has not yet been implemented.

B. The majority of the military is receptive to the repeal.

C. Support of the repeal has been overwhelming.

D. The repeal of the bill was found unconstitutional.

PASSAGE 6

Most video games differ from traditional games like chess or Monopoly in the way they withhold information about the under-lying rules of the system. When you play chess at anything beyond a beginner's level, the rules of the game contain no ambiguity: You know exactly the moves allowed for each piece, the procedures that allow one piece to capture another. The question that con-fronts you sitting down at the chessboard is not: What are the rules here? The question is: What kind of strategy can I concoct that will best exploit those rules to my advantage? In the video game world, on the other hand, the rules are rarely established before you sit down to play. You're given a few basic instructions about how to manipulate objects or characters on the screen and a sense of some kind of objective. But many of the rules become apparent only through exploring the world. You literally learn by playing. This is one reason video games can be frustrating to the non-initiated. You're supposed to figure out what you're supposed to do.

13. What is the best title of the passage?

   A. The Rules of Video Games

   B. Chess Is More Fun Than Monopoly

   C. Video Games Use Exploration

   D. What Am I Supposed to Do?

14. As used in the passage, <u>concoct</u> most nearly means

   A. make up.

   B. blend.

   C. destroy.

   D. borrow.

15. "Non-initiated" refers to people who

   A. love to play chess

   B. have not played video games before

   C. refuse to learn how to play video games

   D. establish the rules to video games

Test Tip

Some inference questions involve the passage as a whole. Others refer to a specific part of the passage. All inference questions want you to think about the facts in the passage.

ANSWERS AND EXPLANATIONS

1. The correct answer is (B). The answer is presented in the first sentence: ". . . the different perspectives" of absentees and managers on absenteeism. The passage doesn't "analyze why *most*" people miss work (A), since it actually states that "most people don't miss much work." The passage never "suggest(s) how to keep workers in the workplace (C)," and its purpose is not to "provide workers with excuses (D)."

2. The correct answer is (D). The passage states that absentees excuse themselves with reasons that are "out of my control." This implies that workers care what their co-workers think of them. Choices (A) and (B) contradict the author of the passage. The author might agree with (C), but you can not make that inference from the passage.

3. The correct answer is (C). The absentees' excuses are not bound by law or lawful acts (A), and choices (B) and (D) are opposites of "legitimate."

4. The correct answer is (A) and is stated in the second sentence. Choices (B) and (C) are not mentioned in the passage. While the passage mentions places where music therapy is often done, it does not state that it "can be done anywhere," even if that is the case.

5. The correct answer is (B). Although the passage describes (A) and (C) and mentions that medical professions accept music therapy as valid and does not dispute that claim, the passage does not describe the process of music therapy.

6. The correct answer is (D). Choices (A), (B), and (C) are mentioned in the passage. "Horseback riding" is not mentioned.

7. The correct answer is (C), highest. Choices (A), (B), and (D) are synonyms for *shear*, but do not fit the meaning of the sentence.

8. The correct answer is (D). The passage does not mention money or profits.

9. The correct answer is (C), "informative." The passage is not entertaining (A), humorous (B), or somber (D).

10. The correct answer is (A), "neutral." The author does not insert any opinion on the subject. The passage is written in a "matter of fact" manner.

11. The correct answer is (C), Bill Clinton.

12. The correct answer is (A) and is stated in the last sentence. The passage does not support choices (B) and (C) as true. Choice (D) confuses the fact that "DADT was found unconstitutional."

13. The correct answer is (C) ("the rules become apparent only through exploring the world").

14. The correct answer is (A), make up or come up with. Choice (B) is a synonym for "concoct," but does not fit the meaning of the sentence. Choices (C) and (D) are opposites.

15. The correct answer is (B), people who "have not played video games before" or someone who is unaccustomed to playing video games.

Mathematics Knowledge

What We'll Cover in This Chapter

- What to Expect on the Mathematics Knowledge Section of the AFQT

- Exercises

- More Practice for the Mathematics Knowledge Section

WHAT TO EXPECT ON THE MATHEMATICS KNOWLEDGE SECTION OF THE AFQT

The AFQT Mathematics Knowledge section measures how well you can solve problems using what you learned in high school math classes. The topics that are typically tested include:

- Number theory

- Numeration

- Algebra operations and equations

- Some basic geometry (angles, triangles; perimeter, area, volume; circumference and area of circles)

- Measurement

- Probability

SOME MATH STRATEGIES

1. Make sure you understand exactly what the question asks you to do.

2. After reading the question, look at the answer choices for clues that will help you.

3. It's a good idea to write your work out, instead of working in your head. That way, it's easier to find any mistakes in your calculations (just in case).

4. If you find that the question is not that easy, try the "plug-in" or "just picking numbers" strategy or the "working backward" strategy (more on both strategies later).

5. Solve the problem. If you have trouble solving the problem, try one of our alternative strategies. For example, the "Work Backward" strategy:

   - Work backward when
     - you are asked to solve an equation
     - you have a word problem
     - the answer choices are numbers
   - Don't work backward when questions
     - have variables in the answer choices
     - don't ask a direct question

6. Quickly check your answers by comparing your answer to the answer choices.

7. If your answer does not match one of the answer choices, make an educated guess. (For the paper-and-pencil test, there is no penalty for wrong answers.)

8. If the question is a hard one, skip it and come back to it later.

STRATEGIES FOR ANSWERING HARD QUESTIONS

Sometimes you might find a word problem confusing, or an equation has so many variables, you're not sure what to do. There are alternative strategies for tackling these problems: plugging in (or picking) an easy number and/or working backward.

PLUGGING IN (OR PICKING) AN EASY NUMBER

You can pick a number when:

- the answer choices contain variables (x, y, or some other letter)

- the question involves percents, fractions, or ratios, but without actual numbers

1. Choose a simple number to replace the variable. Always choose a number that's easy to work with. Choose something small that's easy to manipulate.

2. Plug that easy number into the question. Answer the question.

3. If the answer choices contain numbers, the choice that includes your easy number is the correct one.

4. If the answer choices contain variables, then plug that same easy number into all of the answer choices. The answer choice that is the same as your answer is the right one. If more than one answer choice matches, then you'll have to redo the questions with a different easy number.

Example:

What do you get if you add 4 to *x* and the sum is divided by 2?

A. $\dfrac{4 + x}{2}$

B. $\dfrac{2 + x}{2}$

C. $2 + x$

D. $4 + x$

Pick an easy number. Try 2 (it's always easy). Plug that number into the question. Replace the *x* with 2 and solve. The answer is 3. Plug the easy number into the answer choices and get rid of those that give you an answer different from 3. Answer choice (A) fits:

$$\frac{4 + 2}{2} = 3$$

Test Tip

Remember that not every question is going to be a challenge.

WORKING BACKWARD

1. Start with the answer choice (C).

2. Eliminate answer choices that are too small or too large. That means if answer choice (C) is too small, then the two choices (A) and (B) are too small, also. If answer choice (C) is too large, than answer choice (D) is probably too large, also.

3. Test the answer choice that's left. If it works, then choose that one.

Example:

If $3x - 5 = 10$, then $x =$

    A. 2

    B. 3

    C. 5

    D. 7

ANSWER:

$$3x - 5 = 10$$
$$3x - 5 - 5 = 10 + 5$$
$$3x = 15$$
$$\frac{3x}{3} = \frac{15}{3}$$
$$x = 5$$

Numerical answer choices are usually in order from greatest to least, or vice versa. If you are unsure of how to solve the question and you're plugging in numbers, it makes sense to start with the answer choice (C) and see where that takes you. Even if (C) is the wrong answer, it might give you a clue about what value to plug in next. But don't take too much time!

COMMON MATH TERMINOLOGY AND RULES

Addends add together to create *sums.*

Differences are answers in subtraction.

Products are multiplication answers.

Dividends are divided by **divisors** to get **quotients.**

Commutative Property: The order of operations doesn't matter. You'll find this in addition and multiplication. $2 + 5 = 5 + 2$

Associative Property: You can group items in any way, as in addition and multiplication: $(3 \times 6) \times 2 = 3 \times (6 \times 2)$.

Identity Property of 0: 0 can be added to any number without changing the number.

Identity Property of 1: Any number multiplied by 1 remains the same number.

Order of Operations: PEMDAS. First you have to do the work that's in **P**arentheses and clear the **E**xponents. Then do **M**ultiplication and **D**ivision. **A**ddition and **S**ubtraction are done last.

Integer: Integers are the "counting" numbers, such as 1, 5, 15, and so on, but they also include 0 and the negatives of the counting numbers.

Even Numbers: Even numbers can be evenly divided by 2.

> *Remember that 0 is an even number.*

Odd Numbers: Odd numbers cannot be evenly divided by 2.

Prime Numbers: Prime numbers are divisible only by themselves and 1.

> *The number 1 is **not** a prime number and 2 is the only even prime number.*

These are prime numbers: 2, 3, 5, 7, 11, 13, 17, 19, 23, and so on.

Quotient: This is what you get when you divide two numbers.

Remainder: What's left over when a number is not evenly divisible by another number.

All of the math words on the AFQT have pretty simple definitions. It's just a matter of remembering them well enough to be able to work problems with them. You learned all of this in high school, remember?

FRACTIONS

Fractions are parts of numbers or pieces of the whole. A fraction is a number that looks like this:

$$\frac{a}{b} \text{ (where } a \text{ and } b \text{ are numbers).}$$

The number on top, a, is called the numerator, and the number on the bottom, b, is called the denominator. It's important to remember that fractions are really division problems in disguise. A fraction means you are dividing the numerator by the denominator. The fraction $\frac{a}{b}$ is really the same thing as $a \div b$.

ADDING AND SUBTRACTING FRACTIONS

To add fractions, they have to have the same denominator. If there are only two fractions, you can use cross-multiplication.

Example:

$$\frac{2}{3} + \frac{5}{12}$$

$$\frac{2}{3} \bowtie \frac{5}{12}$$

The easiest way to solve this addition problem is to cross-multiply. So, first multiply the cross products and place them on the top. Then multiply the two bottom numbers and put them on the bottom:

$$\frac{2(12) + 3(5)}{3(12)} = \frac{24 + 15}{36} = \frac{39}{36} = \frac{13}{12} = 1\frac{1}{12}$$

If there are more than two fractions, then you have to find a common denominator. The common denominator is the *smallest* number that each denominator divides into without anything left over.

Example:

$$\text{Add } \frac{1}{2} + \frac{1}{3} + \frac{1}{4} + \frac{1}{5}$$

Here's any easy way to find a common denominator: Choose the biggest denominator number and keep adding that number until you get to a number that is divisible by all of the rest of the denominators (they're really called multiples). If you get stuck, you can multiply all of the bottom numbers together, but the number you end up with is going to be huge.

So for the example above, you get

$$\frac{30}{60} + \frac{20}{60} + \frac{15}{60} + \frac{12}{60} = \frac{77}{60} = 1\frac{17}{60}$$

The numerators are added together to get 77 and this goes on top of the common denominator, 60. Simplify it to get $1\frac{17}{60}$.

After you get the addition of fractions down pat, you'll see that subtraction is done in almost the same way. Remember, instead of adding the numerators together, you have to subtract them.

Example:

$$\frac{4}{5} - \frac{7}{12} = \frac{4(12) - 5(7)}{5(12)} = \frac{48 - 35}{60} = \frac{13}{60}$$

MULTIPLYING AND DIVIDING FRACTIONS

It's easy to multiply fractions: You just multiply across. You can cancel out numbers that are found on both the top and the bottom. And when you want to divide fractions, you just need to multiply by switching the top and bottom in the fraction you're dividing by.

Example:

$\frac{5}{16} \div \frac{5}{8}$ is $\frac{5}{16} \times \frac{8}{5}$. Cross out (or cancel) the two 5's and you get $\frac{8}{16}$ or $\frac{1}{2}$.

Something to Help You Out

When a Number is Divisible by	That Means the
2	last digit will be 0, 2, 4, 6, or 8
3	sum is divisible by 3
4	number you get with the last two digits is divisible by 4
5	last digit is 0 or 5
6	number will be divisible by 2 and 3
8	last three digits of the number make the number divisible by 8

MIXED FRACTIONS

To add or subtract mixed fractions, just find a common denominator. Then you can add or subtract the two fractions. Mixed numbers must be changed into improper fractions so that you can work with them. To multiply or divide mixed numbers, always make them into improper fractions first, then cancel out the factors on the top and the bottom. Multiply what's left over.

EXERCISE 1

1. Determine the sum of $\frac{1}{2} + \frac{2}{3} + \frac{3}{4}$

A. $1\frac{2}{3}$

B. $1\frac{1}{4}$

C. $1\frac{3}{6}$

D. $1\frac{11}{12}$

Answer: (D) $\frac{1}{2} + \frac{2}{3} + \frac{3}{4} = \frac{6}{12} + \frac{8}{12} + \frac{9}{12}$

$$= \frac{23}{12} = 1\frac{11}{12}$$

2. Determine the sum of $\dfrac{5}{15} + \dfrac{3}{30}$

A. $\dfrac{8}{15}$

B. $\dfrac{13}{30}$

C. $\dfrac{15}{30}$

D. $\dfrac{18}{30}$

Answer: (B) $\dfrac{5}{15} + \dfrac{3}{30} = \dfrac{10}{30} + \dfrac{3}{30} = \dfrac{13}{30}$

3. Add $\dfrac{1}{4} + \dfrac{3}{10} + \dfrac{2}{5}$

A. $\dfrac{6}{20}$

B. $\dfrac{8}{20}$

C. $\dfrac{17}{20}$

D. $\dfrac{19}{20}$

Answer: (D) $\dfrac{1}{4} + \dfrac{3}{10} + \dfrac{2}{5} = \dfrac{5}{20} + \dfrac{6}{20} + \dfrac{8}{20} = \dfrac{19}{20}$

FRACTIONS AND DECIMALS

Fractions and decimals are related but different ways to talk about the parts of a whole. A decimal is a number with a decimal point (.). It is really a fraction. The denominator is always 10 (or a power of 10). The number of places (digits) after the decimal point tells you which power of 10 the denominator really is. If there is one digit, the denominator is 10; if there are two digits, the denominator is 100, and so on. Even if there are additional zeros after a digit, the value of the decimal doesn't change:

.6 = .60 = .600, and the other way around, .600 = .60 = .6

Adding decimals

You add decimals the same way that you add whole numbers, as long as you keep the decimal points in a vertical line, one under the other:

Example:

2.34 + .356 + 1.23 + 5.0023

```
  2.3400
  0.3560
  1.2300
+ 5.0023
  8.9283
```

Answer: 8.9283

Subtracting decimals

You subtract decimals the same way you subtract whole numbers, as long as you keep the decimal point in a vertical line, one under the other.

Example:

```
  17.4000
−  3.5432
  13.8568
```

Multiplying and dividing decimals by a power of 10

You multiply decimals the same way you multiply whole numbers. A decimal can be multiplied by a power of 10 by moving the decimal point to the right as may places as the power tells you to. If you multiply by 10, the decimal point is moved one place to the right. If you multiply by 100, the decimal point is moved two places to the right, and so on. A decimal can be divided by a power of 10 by moving the decimal to the left as may places as the power tells you to. If you divide by 10, the decimal point is moved one place to the left. If you divide by 100, the decimal point is moved two places to the left, and so on. If there are not enough places, add zeros in front of the number to make up the difference, and then add a decimal point.

Example:

.5 divided by 10 = .05

.5 divided by 100 = .005

Changing decimals to fractions

Since a decimal point means a number with a denominator is a power of 10, a decimal can be written as a fraction. The numerator is the number itself and the denominator is the power expressed by the number of decimal places in the decimal. So, to change a decimal to a fraction, write the decimal's digits as the numerator and write the decimal's name as the denominator. If you need to, reduce the fraction.

Example:

.020

So, 20 is the numerator, $\dfrac{20}{}$.

Since it's three places to the right, it means thousandths, so 1000 is the denominator, $\dfrac{20}{1000}$.

Reduce by dividing 20 into the top and bottom numbers, $\dfrac{20}{1000} \div \dfrac{20}{20} = \dfrac{1}{50}$.

PERCENTS

The percent symbol (%) means "parts of a hundred." So, 5% is the same as 5 per 100, which is the same as 5/100. As a decimal, it's written as .05. Easy, right? To rewrite a whole number or a decimal as a percent, multiply the number by 100, then add the % sign. To rewrite a fraction or a mixed number as a percent, multiply the fraction or mixed number by 100 and add the % sign. Simplify if you can and add the % sign.

To change a percent to a decimal means moving the decimal two places to the left, because you are really dividing by 100.

$$52\% = .52$$
$$3.4\% = .034$$

These are all **conversions**.

Here's another chart. This one we'll call "The Handy Conversion Chart."

Percent	Decimal	Fraction
10%	.1	$\dfrac{1}{10}$
20%	.2	$\dfrac{1}{5}$
25%	.25	$\dfrac{1}{4}$
30%	.3	$\dfrac{3}{10}$
$33\dfrac{1}{3}\%$	.33	$\dfrac{1}{3}$
40%	.4	$\dfrac{2}{5}$
50%	.5	$\dfrac{1}{2}$
60%	.6	$\dfrac{3}{5}$

(continued)

Percent	Decimal	Fraction
$66\frac{2}{3}\%$	.66	$\frac{2}{3}$
80%	.8	$\frac{4}{5}$
70%	.7	$\frac{7}{10}$
75%	.75	$\frac{3}{4}$
90%	.9	$\frac{9}{10}$

Percent problems are much easier to solve when you plug in 100!

ALGEBRA

You might not even encounter any algebra questions on the test you take. However, if you do, remember that it's the pre-algebra you took early in a high school algebra course. You may have taken pre-algebra as a course in middle school! Pre-algebra includes solving equations, positive and negative numbers, and algebraic expressions.

Algebra uses the same operations as arithmetic: addition, subtraction, multiplication, and division.

ADDITION

If the signs of the numbers are the same, add them and keep the sign. If the signs are different, subtract them and put the sign of the larger number in the answer. Here's an example:

$$4 + -8 = -4$$

Negative 8 is smaller than positive 4, but the value 8 is larger than the value 4, so the answer gets a negative sign.

SUBTRACTION

Subtraction is really addition of the additive inverse. So when you subtract, you only have to change the sign of the number you're subtracting and use the addition rules we discussed above.

$$-4 - (-8) = 4$$

MULTIPLICATION

A negative times a negative equals a positive. If the number of numbers you're multiplying is odd, the negative sign stays.

$$(4)(8) = 32$$
$$(4)(-8) = -32$$
$$(-4)(-8) = 32$$

DIVISION

The same signs equal a positive answer. Different signs equal a negative answer.

$$\frac{32}{8} = 4$$

$$\frac{-32}{4} = -8$$

$$\frac{-32}{-4} = 8$$

$$\frac{32}{-4} = -8$$

EXERCISE 2

1. Find the product of $(-6)(-4)(-4)$ and (-2).

    A. -16

    B. 16

    C. -192

    D. 192

    Answer: $6 \times 4 \times 4 \times 2 = 192$

2. Solve $5a - 4x - 3y$, where $a = -2$, $x = -10$, and $y = 5$.

A. 10

B. 13

C. 15

D. 18

Answer: All you have to do is substitute the numbers for the variables and solve:

$$5(-2) - 4(-10) - 3(5) = -10 + 40 - 15 = 15$$

EQUATIONS

There are rules for solving equations:

1. Remove fractions or decimals using multiplication.

2. Remove the parentheses by using the distributive law, which is to add the numbers in the parentheses and multiply, or distribute, the numbers by each other and then add up those numbers.

3. Isolate the variable on one side of the equal sign.

4. Combine the similar terms. If terms can't be combined, try factoring.

5. Divide by whatever number is next to the variable.

Example:

Solve for x.

$$6x - 3 = 3x + 6 \text{ (Subtract } 3x \text{ from each side.)}$$
$$3x = 9 \text{ (Divide each side by 3.)}$$
$$x = 3$$

When solving algebraic equations, always remember that the order of operations is very important!

Simplify anything that is inside the parentheses. Multiply and divide in order from left to right. Add and subtract in order, from left to right.

FOIL is a multiplication trick to remember:

First

Outer

Inner

Last

Here's another handy chart:

To add a positive and a negative, subtract and take the sign of the number that is farthest from zero on a number line.

To add two negative numbers, just add the numbers and put a negative sign in front of the total.

In multiplication, remember that two negatives make a positive. One of each sign makes a negative.

In division, if the signs are the same, the answer is positive. If the signs are different, the answer is negative.

To solve linear equations, isolate the variable:
- Fractions or decimals: multiply to get rid of them.
- Parentheses: follow the distribution rules.
- Terms that are not similar: try to factor them.
- Coefficients: divide both sides by the coefficient to clear it.

GEOMETRY

There aren't many geometry problems in the Mathematics Knowledge section of the AFQT. You'll probably be asked questions about lines, angles, triangles, squares, rectangles, and circles. More than likely you'll be asked to determine the area or perimeter of a shape, or maybe the size of an angle.

GEOMETRY TERMS TO REMEMBER

Lines

A line equals 180 degrees. Angles next to each other on a line must add up to 180 degrees.

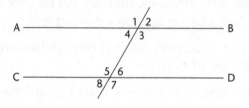

Parallel lines that are cut by another line form related angles. Opposite angles are always equal to each other.

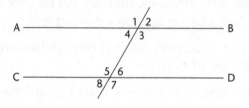

In the picture above, if

$\overline{AB}$ is parallel to $\overline{CD}$, then:

$$\angle 1 = \angle 3, \angle 5, \text{ and } \angle 7$$
$$\angle 2 = \angle 4, \angle 6, \text{ and } \angle 8$$

A bisector cuts objects into two equal pieces.

Squares: formulas

A square has four equal sides and looks like this:

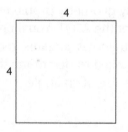

Each angle in a square is 90° and they add up to 360°.

Perimeter of Square = 4*s*. Simply put, multiply one side by 4 to find the perimeter. That's also the same as adding all of the sides. They're all equal.

Area of Square = s^2. Just square one side. That's the same as length × width.

Rectangles: formulas

A rectangle looks like this:

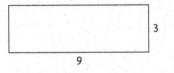

Perimeter of Rectangle = sum of 4 sides = *l* + *l* + *w* + *w* = 2*l* + 2*w* or, in other words, just add the sides.

Area of Rectangle = *l* × *w*. Multiply the two sides next to each other. As in a square, each angle in a rectangle is 90° and they add up to 360°.

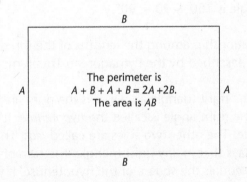

Squares and rectangles have four 90° angles in each corner. The sum of the four angles is 360°.

Triangles

There are many types of triangles, but they all have three sides and three angles.

Perimeter of triangle = the sum of the three sides

Area of triangle $= \dfrac{1}{2} bh$ (b is the base of the triangle and h is the height). The measures of all the angles in a triangle add up to 180°. And, if opposite angles are equal, so are the opposite sides; and if the opposite sides are equal, so are the opposite angles.

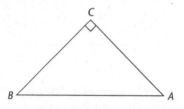

A right triangle is one in which one of the three angles is a *right angle* that measures 90°. The right angle is identified by a little "box" in the triangle. Since the sum of all three of the angles in any triangle equals 180°, the sum of the two remaining angles in a right triangle is 180 − 90 = 90°.

The relationship among the lengths of the three sides of a right triangle is described by the Pythagorean Theorem: $a^2 + b^2 = c^2$.

Using the right triangle above, C is the right angle. The side opposite the right angle is called the *hypotenuse*. It's always the longest side. The other two sides are called *legs*. The Pythagorean Theorem says that in any right triangle, the sum of the squares of the legs equals the square of the hypotenuse. If you know the lengths of any two sides of a right triangle, you can figure out the length of the third side.

> *Remember: the third side of a triangle can never be greater than the sum or smaller than the difference of the other two sides. That means if you subtract two side lengths, the third side must be larger than that difference.*

Circles

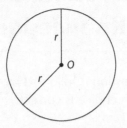

The radius of a circle is a line from the center to the edge, and the distance from any point on the circle to the center is expressed by *r*.

The diameter is a line through the center across a circle, and it is twice the radius.

Diameter = 2*r*

Circumference = (π)*d*

Area = (π) • *r²*

SO, WHAT'S THE PLAN?

Now that you've got the tools, let's see how well you use them. The Mathematics Knowledge section of the AFQT includes 25 questions to measure your understanding of mathematical concepts, principles, and procedures. Take the following practice test under real test conditions; that is to say, allow 24 minutes to complete the 25 questions.

Numerical answer choices are usually in order from greatest to least, or the other way around. If you are plugging in numbers, it makes sense to start with answer choice (C) and see where it takes you. Even if (C) is the wrong answer, it may help show you what value to plug in next.

You can now begin the test.

Practice Set: Mathematics Knowledge

Directions: Each question is followed by four possible answers choices. Decide which choice is correct.

1. What is 44% of 25?
   A. 7
   B. 9
   C. 11
   D. 13

2. If a box of pencils measures 8 inches by 3 inches by 1 inch, how many boxes will fit in a carton that measures 24 inches by 32 inches by 12 inches?
   A. 24
   B. 48
   C. 144
   D. 384

3. If 25x = 450, what is the value of 5x?
   A. 125
   B. 90
   C. 45
   D. 9

4.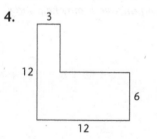

   If all of the angles in the above figure are right angles, what is the area of the figure?

A. 48

B. 64

C. 72

D. 90

5. The average of 6 numbers is 5. If the sum of all but one of these numbers is 23, what is the value of the final number?

A. 2

B. 3

C. 5

D. 7

6. If $\dfrac{x}{4} = \dfrac{12}{8}$, what is the value of x?

A. 4

B. 6

C. 8

D. 12

7. $\dfrac{40 \times 30 \times 20}{8 \times 6 \times 4} =$

A. 25

B. 125

C. 250

D. 300

8. What percent of $\dfrac{5}{6}$ is $\dfrac{3}{4}$?

A. 60%

B. 75%

C. 80%

D. 90%

9. 200% of 800 =

  A. 200

  B. 400

  C. 1600

  D. 10,000

10. If $6x - (2x+6) = x + 3$, then $x =$

  A. -3

  B. -2

  C. 3

  D. 2

11. What kind of polygon is the following figure?

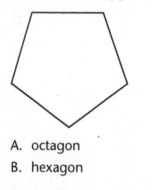

  A. octagon   C. heptagon

  B. hexagon   D. pentagon

12. If the perimeter of a rectangle is 68 yards and the width is 48 feet, the length is

  A. 18 yards.

  B. 24 yards.

  C. 18 feet.

  D. 16 feet.

13. The difference between 306,842 and 215,702 =

  A. 90,407

  B. 91,140

  C. 89,723

  D. 88,392

14. What will it cost to carpet a room 12 ft. wide and 15 ft. long if the carpet costs $20.00 per square yard?

   A. $244.00

   B. $350.00

   C. $398.00

   D. $400.00

15. $\frac{5}{12}$ is equal to what percent?

   A. 41%

   B. $41\frac{2}{3}\%$

   C. 4.1%

   D. $41\frac{1}{3}\%$

16. What percent of 48 is 48?

   A. 1

   B. 10

   C. 100

   D. 148

17. Solve for x: $3x - 2 = 3 + 2x$

   A. 1

   B. 5

   C. −1

   D. −5

18. What is the percent value of $\frac{1}{2}$?

   A. 10%

   B. 20%

   C. 50%

   D. 2%

19. $\frac{1}{2} \times 32 \times \frac{3}{8} =$

    A. 2

    B. 6

    C. 8

    D. 16

20. What is another way to write 12^2?

    A. 24

    B. 122

    C. 144

    D. 164

21. $0.80 =$

    A. $\frac{4}{5}$

    B. $\frac{1}{4}$

    C. $\frac{1}{8}$

    D. $\frac{2}{5}$

22. $2.75 =$

    A. $2\frac{3}{4}$

    B. $2\frac{7}{5}$

    C. $2\frac{5}{7}$

    D. $\frac{2}{75}$

23. 35% of what number is equal to 70?

    A. 100

    B. 200

    C. 300

    D. 700

24. What is the area of △DEF?

    A. 2

    B. 4

    C. 6

    D. 8

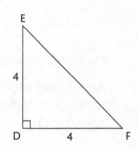

25. $b - 3 > 7$

    A. $b < 10$

    B. $b > 10$

    C. $b < 7$

    D. $b < 3$

ANSWERS AND EXPLANATIONS

1. (C) $(.44) \times 25 = 11$

2. (D) Divide the volume of the carton by the volume of one box:

$$\frac{24 \times 32 \times 12}{8 \times 3 \times 1}$$

If you rearrange the fraction to make it easier to factor:

$$\frac{32 \times 24 \times 12}{8 \times 3 \times 1} = \frac{4 \times 8 \times 12}{1 \times 1 \times 1} = \frac{384}{1} = 384 \text{ boxes of pencils}$$

3. (B) $5x$ is $\frac{1}{5}$ of $25x$, so it must equal 1/5 of 450, which is 90. You don't need to solve for x.

4. (D) If you divide the figure into two rectangles, it's easier to solve.

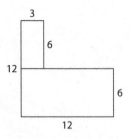

Now find the area of each rectangle and add them together:

Area (upper rectangle) = $3 \times 6 = 18$
Area (lower rectangle) = $6 \times 12 = 72$
Area (total)   = $72 + 18 = 90$

5. (D) The average of 6 numbers is 5, so the sum of all 6 numbers is 30. If the sum of all but 1 is 23, then the missing number must be $30 - 23$, or 7.

6. (B) $\dfrac{x}{4} = \dfrac{12}{8}$

$\dfrac{8x}{8} = \dfrac{48}{8}$

$x = 6$

7. (B) Instead of doing long multiplication and division, it's much easier if you cancel as much as you can:

$$\frac{40 \times 30 \times 20}{8 \times 6 \times 4} = \frac{5 \times 5 \times 5}{1 \times 1 \times 1} = 5 \times 5 \times 5 = 125$$

8. (D) $\dfrac{3}{4} \div \dfrac{5}{6} =$

$\dfrac{3}{4} \times \dfrac{6}{5} =$

$= \dfrac{18}{20} = \dfrac{9}{10} = .9 = 90\%$

9. (C) 200% of 800 = 2.00 × 800 = 1600

10. (C) 6x − (2x + 6) = x + 3

6x − 2x − 6 = x + 3

4x − 6 = x + 3

$$\frac{-x}{3x - 6} = \frac{-x}{3}$$

$$\frac{+6}{\frac{3x}{3}} = \frac{+6}{\frac{9}{3}}$$

x = 3

11. (D) A five-sided polygon is a pentagon.

12. (A) Perimeter = 2(l + w)

In this question, length = x yards

Each width = 48 ft ÷ 3

= 16 yards

2(x + 16) = 68

2x + 32 = 68

$$\frac{-32}{\frac{2x}{2}} = \frac{-32}{\frac{36}{2}}$$

x = 18

13. (B)

306,842
−215,702
91,140

14. (D)

12 feet = 4 yards

15 feet = 5 yards

4 yards × 5 yards = 20 square yards

$20.00 per sq.yd

$$\frac{\times\ 20}{\$400.00}\ \text{sq.yards}$$

15. (B) Multiply by 100:

$$\frac{5}{12} \times 100 = \frac{125}{3} = 41\frac{2}{3}\%$$

16. (C) $\dfrac{48}{48} = 1 = 100\%$

17. (B)

$3x - 2 = 3 + 2x$

$x = 5$

18. (C) 50%

19. (B)

$$\frac{1}{2} \times 32 \times \frac{3}{8} = 16 \times \frac{3}{8} = 6$$

20. (C) $12^2 = 12 \times 12 = 144$

21. (A) $0.80 = \dfrac{4}{5}$

22. (A) The number 2.75 has a whole number, plus a fraction of a number. $.75 = \dfrac{3}{4}$, add the whole number, 2 to the fraction $= 2\dfrac{3}{4}$

23. (B) 200. Divide 70 by 35, then multiply the answer by 100.

24. (D) Area $= \dfrac{1}{2} \times 4 \times 4 = 8$

25. (B)

$b - 3 > 7$

$b - 3 + 3 > 7 + 3$

$b > 10$

Arithmetic Reasoning

WHAT TO EXPECT ON THE ARITHMETIC REASONING SECTION OF THE AFQT

The arithmetic reasoning section tests how well you can solve **word problems** by measuring your ability to solve mathematical calculations that come from basic, simple word problems. You may not realize it, but word problems are just real-life situations that involve math. Here's an example:

If a pair of combat boots that normally sells for $50 is now on sale for 50% off the original price, how much does the pair of boots cost?

If you *translate* the problem into *50% of $50 equals $25,* then you know that the boots now cost $25. **Translation** is important when you need to solve word problems. (More on translations later.)

The Arithmetic Reasoning section contains 30 questions and you'll have 30 minutes to answer the questions. The questions require you to read a word problem, figure out what the question is asking (there's that translation again), and choose the correct answer. The types of arithmetic word problems you'll likely see are numbers and number relationships, ratio and proportion, percent, percent change, measurement, motion, and simple interest.

UNDERSTANDING TRANSLATIONS

A word problem can test any kind of math, such as arithmetic, fractions, decimals, percentages, and some algebra and geometry. "Translating" in math means that when you read a word problem, you need to translate the English sentence into a math sentence. Translating into math will help you put a word problem into math terms so that you can easily find the solution to the problem.

You may not realize it, but you've been dealing with lots of word problems while in school and out of school. Sure, you've seen them on tests, but did you know that word problems are just real-life situations? Word problems do relate to your everyday life—in or out of the classroom!

The following chart gives you some terms that appear frequently in word problems. You probably remember most, if not all of them.

The translation chart is a good reference to keep handy while you practice.

English	Math	Example	Translation
a number, what	x, n, p	Two more than a number is 6.	$n + 2 = 6$
equals, is, are, was, has, costs	$=$	Private Smith is 18 years old.	$s = 18$
		A hat costs $24.	$h = 24$

Continued →

(Continued from previous page)

English	Math	Example	Translation
sum, more, more than, greater, added to, total, altogether, increased by, older than	+	Jim has three more DVDs than the PX sells.	$j = p + 3$
		Jim and the PX have a total of 200 DVDs.	$j + p = 200$
		Kim is two years older than Tom.	$k = 2 + t$
difference, fewer, less than, decreased by, younger than, left over	−	The difference between the two numbers is 16. Tom is two years younger than Kim.	$x - y = 16$ $t = k - 2$
of, times, product of, twice	×	Thirty percent of Bob's CDs are from the 90s.	$0.30 \times c$
		Half of the platoon is from California.	$\frac{1}{2} \times p$
		The product of the two numbers is 14.	$a \times b = 14$
per, divided by, for, out of		Add 2 cups per gallon.	2 cups/gallon
		The jeep gets 8 miles per gallon.	8 miles/gallon

LOST IN TRANSLATION?

Translating might seem a little strange at first, but we assure you it's easy, once you think logically. First, you use the first letter of the **unknown** as the variable.

> *Attention: Don't use the same variable (letter) to stand for more than one unknown.*

Second, translate the information that the word problem gives you, step by step, piece by piece. Make sure you don't make the mistake of translating illogically. Check out how easy it is to make a mistake in translation if you don't think logically and aren't paying attention.

Example:

Translate this statement:

The sergeant has five fewer commendations than the lieutenant.

Incorrect Translation: $s - 5 = l$

This is incorrect because you can't translate from left to right without thinking logically first. Remember the translation chart? The word "has" translates into = (or "equals"). The mistake made above is that the word "has" was translated into a − (or "minus" sign) and the word "than" was translated into an = (or "equals" sign).

Correct Translation: $s = l - 5$, where the sergeant $s = 5$ fewer commendations, $l - 5$, than the lieutenant, $s = l - 5$.

1. Read the word problem completely.

2. Figure out what the problem is asking you to do.

3. Set up your math equations based on your translation.

4. Solve the problem.

5. Choose the correct answer (since it's a multiple-choice test).

FIGURE THE PROBLEM OUT

When you translate word problems, you'll come across a lot of math terms. Here's another chart to keep handy when you practice.

Clue Words	What to Do	Examples
Sum	Add	If the sum of the bunks is
Total	Add	The total number is
In all	Add	How many in all?
Added	Add	If *x* is added to *y*
Increased by	Add	If the size is increased by
Plus	Add	The interest plus the principal is
More than	Add	If the DVDs cost $10 more than
Less than	Subtract	The total was less than
Fewer than	Subtract	If there are 50 fewer recruits than
Difference	Subtract	If the difference in the number is
Minus	Subtract	*x* minus *y*
Times	Multiply	If there are 5 times as many books as
Product	Multiply	The product of *x* and *y* is
At	Multiply	Two sleeping bags at $30 per bag
Per	Multiply	Two sleeping bags at $30 per bag
Total	Multiply	He spent $10 a day on cigarettes for a total of four weeks.
Quotient	Divide	What is the quotient if the denominator is 400?
Divided into/ equally	Divide	The marines were divided into
Ratio	Divide	If the ratio of goods to services is
Percent	Divide	What percent of *a* is *b*?
Is	Equals	If she spent $55 in one store and $25 in the restaurant, her total spending is
Sells for	Equals	If the backpack sells for *x* dollars

Remember when you translate to start by assigning the variables. If the problem sentence says "number," let n stand for "number." If the problem asks for the "product," remember that means "multiply." If the problem sentence says "is equal to," that simply means, "=" (the "equals" sign).

> Attention: **Sum** is the result of addition. **Difference** is the result of subtraction. **Product** is the result of multiplication. **Quotient** is the result of division.

EXERCISE 1

Now fill in the math equivalents for these sentences.

English Sentence	Math Equation
1. Cecily has three dollars less than Tom.	
2. Tim has two pencils for every pencil John has.	
3. The ratio of Robert's AFQT score to Donna's score is. . .	
4. The sum of Robert's and Maria's income is $100 less than twice Maria's income.	

ANSWERS

1. $C = T - 3$
2. $\dfrac{T}{J} = \dfrac{2}{1}$
3. $\dfrac{R}{D}$
4. $R + M = 2M - 100$

Test Tip

In some of the questions, you might find that the numbers are buried in a story that begs for a translation. Don't be sidetracked by the little details—pay attention to the numbers!

EXERCISE 2

1. Two more than three times a number is 20. What is the number?

   A. 2

   B. 4

   C. 6

   D. 18

2. A boat traveled at 24 miles per hour for 3 hours. How many total miles did the boat travel?

   A. 12

   B. 18

   C. 27

   D. 72

3. On a certain team, there are 14 boys and 6 girls. What is the ratio of boys to girls?

   A. 3:7

   B. 4:7

   C. 14:3

   D. 7:3

4. How many 12-passenger vans will it take to transport 120 soldiers?

   A. 10

   B. 12

   C. 14

   D. 16

EXERCISE 2 ANSWERS

1. (C). Make the number n. "Three times a number" means $3n$. So 2 more than that is $3n + 2$. "Is 20" means $= 20$.

$$3n + 2 = 20$$
$$3n = 18$$
$$n = 6$$

2. (D). $\dfrac{24 \text{ miles}}{1 \text{ hour}} \times 3 \text{ hours} = 72 \text{ miles}$

3. (D). Set up the ratio as a fraction, which is $\dfrac{14}{6}$. Make sure you express the fraction in its lowest terms by dividing the numerator and the denominator by the greatest common factor: 2. So, $\dfrac{14}{6} = \dfrac{7}{3}$.

4. (A). $\dfrac{120}{12} = 10$ or 10 soldiers per van

Test Tip

Always make sure the things you're comparing are in the same unit. If not, convert one so that they are in the same unit.

WORD PROBLEMS WITH FRACTIONS

You probably don't think about it, but you use fractions all the time. When you say "the Los Angeles Clippers won one-half of their games last year" or when you "cut that fabric in half," you're using fractions. When you work with fractions, you must remember that the number at the top of the fraction (on top of the fraction bar) is the numerator and the number at the bottom (of the fraction bar) is the denominator and represents the whole (thing). Remember when you first learned about fractions? The lesson most likely described fractions in terms of a pie. If the whole number is the entire pie, than a fraction is a piece of that pie and represents a piece of the whole. For example: You slice the pie into 6 equal pieces. You ate 5 of the pieces. You ate $\dfrac{5}{6}$ of the entire pie and left $\dfrac{1}{6}$ in the pan. Easy.

Attention: The top of a fraction is called the numerator.
The bottom of a fraction is called the denominator.

RATIOS AND PROPORTIONS

Ratios are a way to compare things that is very useful in everyday life. You talk about the ratio of privates to sergeants or the ratio of men to women or the ratio of questions you answered correctly to those you missed, and so on. On the AFQT, you will almost certainly see word problems that require you to work with ratios and proportions.

When two ratios are equal to each other, they are **in proportion** to each other, or proportional. If the value of one of the two ratios is unknown, you can find it by making the ratios equal to each other and then **cross-multiplying** to find the answer.

Example: Harry, an author, writes an average of 100 pages per week. How many weeks will it take him to write 2,000 pages?

Translate: How long (weeks) will it take him to write 2,000 pages?

You know that he writes 100 pages in a week and there are 2,000 pages that he needs to write.

Here's your proportion:

$$\frac{\text{Number of pages}}{1 \text{ week}} = \frac{\text{number of pages}}{x \text{ weeks}}$$

which looks like this:

$$\frac{100 \text{ pages}}{1 \text{ week}} = \frac{2,000 \text{ pages}}{x \text{ weeks}}$$

Multiply:

$$100x = 2,000$$
$$x = 20$$

So, it takes the author 20 weeks to write 2,000 pages.

Remember: When you set up a proportion, make sure you put the pieces of the proportion in the same place in each ratio. You'll usually encounter the following ratios: inches/feet; feet/yards; hours/minutes; minutes/seconds; ounces/pounds.

EXERCISE 3

1. If Captain Jones runs 3 miles in 40 minutes, how many miles would he run in 2 hours?

   A. 5

   B. 8

   C. 9

   D. 15

2. Ramon's car uses 20 gallons of gas to drive 425 miles. At this rate, approximately how many gallons of gas will he need for a trip of 1,000 miles?

   A. 42

   B. 45

   C. 46

   D. 47

3. On a map, ½ inch = 10 miles. How many miles apart are two towns that are 2¼ inches apart on the map?

   A. 42

   B. 44

   C. 45

   D. 47

4. A gear that has 20 teeth turning at 200 revolutions per minute is combined with a second gear that turns at 250 revolutions per minute. How many teeth does the second gear have?

   A. 16

   B. 18

   C. 20

   D. 25

5. A deli served 300 customers during a 12-hour day. At what rate did the deli serve customers?

   A. 15 per hr

   B. 25 per hr

   C. 30 per hr

   D. 60 per hr

EXERCISE 3 ANSWERS

1. (C). Note that one ratio talks about time in minutes and one in hours. Before you set up the proportion, make the units the same. The first ratio is $\dfrac{3 \text{ miles}}{40 \text{ minutes}}$. Since the number of miles she ran is on the top of the first ratio, it should be on top in the second ratio. We'll make the number of miles run in 2 hours x. Because there are 60 minutes in an hour, we'll say $2(60) = 120$ minutes in 2 hours. So, the second ratio is $\dfrac{x \text{ miles}}{120 \text{ minutes}}$.

   Make the two ratios equal and cross-multiply to solve x.

   $$\frac{3 \text{ miles}}{40 \text{ minutes}} = \frac{x \text{ miles}}{120 \text{ minutes}}$$
   $$40x = (3)(120)$$
   $$40x = 360$$
   $$x = 9$$

2. (D).
   $$\frac{20 \text{ gal}}{425 \text{ miles}} = \frac{x}{1{,}000 \text{ miles}}$$
   $$425x = 20{,}000$$
   $$17x = 800 \text{ (Divide by 25)}$$
   $$x = 47\frac{1}{17}$$

3. (C).
   $$\frac{\frac{1}{2} \text{ inches}}{10} = \frac{2\frac{1}{4}}{x}$$
   $$\frac{1}{2}x = 22\frac{1}{2}$$
   $$x = 45$$

4. (A).

$$20 \times 200 = x \text{ (times) } 250$$
$$250x = 4{,}000$$
$$x = 16$$

5. (B). $\dfrac{\text{customers served}}{\text{hours}} = \dfrac{300}{12}$

$$x = 25$$

PERCENTS

Percent means "per 100." A percent is a fraction with a denominator of 100. For example, 20% is the same as $\dfrac{20}{100}$ or $\dfrac{2}{10}$ or $\dfrac{1}{5}$. Remember that percents can also be written as decimals: 20% = .20.

The AFQT Arithmetic Reasoning section may have questions that deal with percents. The formula you'll need to learn is

$$\text{Percent} \times \text{whole} = \text{part}$$

(Or, part/whole = %/100).

If you know two of the three "pieces," you can plug them into the formula to find the third "piece."

> *"Percent" is the number with the percent symbol (%) after it. "Whole" is the "total." "How many" is the unknown you must find.*

Example:

The sale at the sporting goods store is 25% off the regular prices in the entire store. If you save $12.75 on the soccer shoes you bought, what is the regular price of the shoes (no tax was applied)?

So, the percent is 25% and $12.75 is the part. The "whole" is the "total" price of the shoes before they were reduced.

$$\text{Percent} \times \text{whole} = \text{part}$$
$$25\% \times \text{whole} = \$12.75$$
$$.25 \times \text{whole} = \$12.75$$
$$\text{whole} = \frac{\$12.75}{.25}$$
$$\text{whole} = \$51.00$$

EXERCISE 4

1. In a collection of 250 ceramic chess pieces, 30% of the pieces were made before 1920. How many of the chess pieces were made before 1920?

   A. 25

   B. 30

   C. 50

   D. 75

2. People's Airline has flights that cost 30% less than the normal fare. If the normal fare from New York to Chicago is $450, how much would the discounted flight cost?

   A. $115

   B. $135

   C. $315

   D. $450

3. Private Smith received a salary raise from $25,000 to $27,500. What was the percentage of the salary increase?

   A. 10%

   B. 12%

   C. 15%

   D. 20%

4. Mike read 70% of the magazine articles that his best friend had written. If he read 14 articles, how many articles had his friend written?

   A. 7

   B. 10

   C. 15

   D. 20

5. The population of Town B has increased from 80,000 residents to 100,000 residents in the past 10 years. What is the percent of increase?

   A. 10%

   B. 25%

   C. 30%

   D. 50%

EXERCISE 4 ANSWERS

1. (D). Have x represent the number of chess pieces.

$$\frac{\text{Part}}{\text{whole}} = \frac{\%}{100}$$

$$\frac{x}{250} = \frac{30}{100}$$

$$\frac{x}{250} = \frac{3}{10}$$

$$10x = 3(250)$$

$$\frac{10x}{10} = \frac{750}{10}$$

$$x = 75$$

2. (C). The discount is 30% of $450.

$$\frac{x}{450} = \frac{30}{100}$$

$$\frac{x}{450} = \frac{3}{10}$$

$$10x = 3(450)$$

$$\frac{10x}{10} = \frac{1,350}{10} \text{ (Cross-multiply.)}$$

$$x = \$135 \text{ (This is the discount.)}$$

Now, subtract $135 from $450 (the normal fare) to get the discounted fare.

$$\$450.00 - \$135.00 = \$315.00$$

3. (A). Percent of increase = amount of increase/original

$27,500 − $25,000 = $2,500 (Amount of increase)

$$x = \frac{2,500}{25,000} = \frac{1}{10}$$

$$x = .10, \text{ or } 10\%$$

4. (D). %/100 = part/whole

$$\frac{70}{100} = \frac{14}{a}$$

$$0.70 = \frac{14}{a} \text{ (Cross-multiply)}$$

$$0.70a = 14$$

$$a = 20$$

5. (B). Subtract 80,000 from 100,000 to find the amount of increase = 20,000

$$\text{Percent of increase} = \frac{20,000}{80,000} = \frac{1}{4}$$

$$\frac{1}{4} = .25, \text{ or } 25\%$$

MOTION WORD PROBLEMS

Motion problems involve vehicles traveling an amount of time, at some speed, covering a distance. You remember those. There's a formula you need to use to solve motion problems:

Rate × Time = Distance, or $R \times T = D$

Again, if you have two of the pieces, you can plug those pieces into the formula.

Example:

Jean drives 5 hours and travels a distance of 350 miles. At what speed did Jean drive?

You know that it took Jean 5 hours—that is the time, or **T**. You also know that she drove a distance of 350 miles—that is the distance, or **D**. Since you know the time and the distance, you can easily determine how fast she was driving—the rate of speed, or **R**.

$$R \times T = D$$
$$R \times 5 = 350$$
$$R \times \frac{5}{5} = \frac{350}{5}$$
$$R = 70$$

Jean drove at a speed of 70 miles per hour.

EXERCISE 5

1. Mel drives 240 miles at 40 miles per hour. If he drove this distance at 60 miles per hour, how much less time would his trip take?

   A. 1 hour

   B. 2 hours

   C. 4 hours

   D. 6 hours

Test Tip *Don't forget to solve the entire problem!*

2. If an athlete runs 2 miles in 13.5 minutes, how many minutes per mile did he run?

   A. 6.5 minutes

   B. 6.75 minutes

   C. 7 minutes

   D. 8 minutes

3. If Peter drives to the base from his house at an average of 55 miles per hour, it would take him 3 hours to get to the base. How many miles is it from Peter's house to the base?

   A. 154

   B. 165

   C. 170

   D. 186

4. The Amtrak train ride from Princeton Junction to Logan takes 5.5 hours. If the train travels at a speed of 60 miles per hour, how many miles is it traveling?

   A. 200

   B. 230

   C. 300

   D. 330

5. Denise walked 20 miles in 5 hours. What was her average speed?

   A. 4.0 miles per hour

   B. 4.5 miles per hour

   C. 5.0 miles per hour

   D. 5.6 miles per hour

EXERCISE 5 ANSWERS

1. (B). Mel can get there faster.

$$D = 240$$
$$R = 40$$

Since $R \times T = D$,

$$40 \times T = 240$$
$$T = 6$$

So, it takes him 6 hours to drive 240 miles at 40 miles per hour. But:

$$60 \times T = 240$$
$$T = 4$$

If he drove 60 miles per hour for 240 miles, it would take him 4 hours. The question asks "how much *less* time would his trip take?"

$$6 \text{ hours} - 4 \text{ hours} = 2 \text{ hours}$$

2. (B). $R \times T = D$

$$R \times 13.5 \text{ minutes} = 2 \text{ miles}$$
$$R = \frac{13.5}{2}$$
$$R = 6.75$$

3. (B). $R \times T = D$

$$55 \times 3 = D$$
$$165 = D$$

4. (D). $R \times T = D$

$$60 \times 5.5 = D$$
$$330 = D$$

5. (A). $R \times T = D$

$$R \times 5 = 20$$
$$R = 4$$

GEOMETRY WORD PROBLEMS

The AFQT Arithmetic Reasoning section may also test your geometry skills. You've had plenty of practice in high school, so don't worry. Today, we use geometry in almost every line of work and it is the first math you learn in school that deals with shapes. The geometry questions in the Arithmetic Reasoning section will deal with perimeter, area, and volume of shapes like rectangles, squares, or circles. To answer them, all you need to do is be able to translate the information the problem provides using some facts about the figures. You might need to use information about the units of measure that we went over in more detail in the Math Knowledge chapter.

Test Tip

Translate geometry word problems carefully. Make sure you plug the variables into the correct formula.

Example:

Corporal Jones is buying wood to make a rectangular picture frame that will measure 8 inches by 11 inches. The wood costs 10 cents per inch. How much will Cpl. Jones have to pay for the wood?

Length of wood needed for rectangle: 2 × length + 2 × width

2(11) + 2(8) = 38 inches (Length of wood)

If each inch costs $0.10, then 0.10 × 38 = $3.80.

EXERCISE 6

1. A farmer wants to fertilize his 40-foot by 50-foot garden. If one bag of fertilizer covers 20 square feet, how many bags of fertilizer does he need to cover the whole garden?

   A. 100

   B. 170

   C. 190

   D. 1,500

2. Toni wants to build a fence around her yard. Her yard measures 35 feet by 65 feet. How many feet of fence does she need?

A. 100

B. 200

C. 500

D. 2,175

EXERCISE 6 ANSWERS

1. (A). First calculate the area of the garden:

$$Area = length \times width$$
$$A = l \times w$$
$$A = 40 \times 50$$
$$A = 2,000$$

Then figure out how many bags of fertilizer the farmer needs:

$$2,000 \text{ square feet} \times \frac{1 \text{ bag}}{20 \text{ square feet}} = 100 \text{ bags}$$

2. (B). You have to find the perimeter of the yard.
Perimeter = $2 \times l + 2 \times w$

$$P = 2l + 2w$$
$$P = 2(35) + 2(65)$$
$$P = 70 + 130$$
$$P = 200$$

Remember to use common sense! Does your answer seem reasonable?

SIMPLE INTEREST

Interest is a charge for money that you borrowed or the money that you earned from an investment. In simple-interest word problems, the interest is always calculated on the original amount of money. The formula you need to calculate simple interest is

Interest = Principal × Rate × Time, or *I* = *prt*

Example:

Alice invested $10,000 into an annuity that yields 5% interest each year. If she leaves the money in for 4 years, how much interest will she earn?

The principal is the original amount of money invested: $10,000.

The rate is the percent amount by which the interest is paid: 5%.

The time is how long she leaves the money in: 4 years.

So, using the formula:

$$I = 10,000 \times 0.05 \times 4$$
$$I = \$2,000$$

Test Tip *Make sure you read the question carefully. Sometimes the question may require more steps to solve the problem.*

Here's one for you to try. The problems on the AFQT are pretty straightforward.

1. Robert deposited $3,000 in an investment for 5 years. If he earned $300 interest during the 5 years, what was the interest rate each year?

    A. 5%

    B. 4%

    C. 3%

    D. 2%

(D). $I = prt$

$$300 = (3,000)(r)(5)$$
$$300 = 15,000r$$
$$\frac{300}{15,000} = \frac{15,000r}{1,500}$$
$$.02 = r$$
$$2\% = r$$

Things to remember to make your Arithmetic Reasoning experience easier:

1. Translating English to math allows you to place the word problem into a mathematical "sentence."

2. Always read the word problem carefully to make sure you are answering what is being asked.

3. Learn the math "vocabulary" such as: "of" means multiplication; "is" means equal; "what" means a variable; "what percent" means $\frac{x}{100}$.

4. Remember your formulas!

5. Read the question carefully and answer completely.

SO, WHAT'S THE PLAN?

Now that you've got the tools, let's see how well you use them. The Arithmetic Reasoning section of the AFQT includes arithmetic word problems. Take the following practice test under real test conditions; that is, allow 36 minutes to complete the 30 questions.

Test Tip

If you want to raise your score, you need to make sure you read the question carefully before you start calculating. Then read the question again before you choose the answer.

You can now begin the test.

Practice Set: Arithmetic Reasoning

Directions: Each question is followed by four possible answer choices. Decide which choice is correct.

1. Anthony spent $4.50 for a movie on demand. This represents $\frac{3}{4}$ of his allowance for the week. What did he have left that week?
   A. $1.00
   B. $1.25
   C. $1.50
   D. $1.75

2. If Kathy rides her bike at a constant speed of 15 miles per hour, how many minutes will it take for her to ride $\frac{1}{2}$ mile?
   A. 2 minutes
   B. 4 minutes
   C. 15 minutes
   D. 30 minutes

3. Fourteen recruits come to practice. If that represents $\frac{7}{8}$ of the team, what is the total number of team members?
   A. 12
   B. 16
   C. 20
   D. 24

4. If two pairs of shoes cost $52.00, what is the cost of 10 pairs of shoes at this rate?
   A. $104
   B. $160
   C. $210
   D. $260

5. The bookstore gives a 10% discount to military personnel. What would a service member actually pay for a book that costs $24.00?

   A. $15.45

   B. $16.60

   C. $19.65

   D. $21.60

6. A carpenter needs four lengths of wood, each 3 feet 6 inches long. Wood is sold by the foot. How many feet does he need?

   A. 12

   B. 14

   C. 16

   D. 17

7. Sixty percent of the students in a class are boys. If 12 of the students in the class are girls, what is the total number of students in the class?

   A. 18

   B. 24

   C. 30

   D. 40

8. A company had 600 employees. It laid off 68 of them, then hired back 45 of those it had laid off. How many employees does the company now have?

   A. 600

   B. 587

   C. 577

   D. 532

9. According to a particular recipe, 20 pounds of sugar are needed to make 500 cupcakes. At this rate, how many pounds of sugar are needed to make 25 cupcakes?

   A. 1

   B. 3

   C. 5

   D. 6

10. A picture is 8 inches wide and 10 inches long. If it is enlarged so that the new length is 25 inches, what will the new width be?

    A. $16\frac{1}{2}$

    B. 18

    C. 20

    D. $21\frac{1}{2}$

11. This month, Cecil has used 260 minutes on his cell phone. If he has $\frac{12}{25}$ of the minutes on his monthly plan limit left, what is the total number of minutes in his monthly plan limit?

    A. 100

    B. 300

    C. 500

    D. 600

12. Regina has 4 fewer vacation days than Thomas does. Regina used ½ her vacation days on a trip. How many vacation days did Regina use if Thomas has 18 vacation days?

    A. 4

    B. 5

    C. 6

    D. 7

13. At the local library, there are 8 shelves of books with a total of 128 books. What is the average number of books per bookshelf?

    A. 4

    B. 6

    C. 12

    D. 16

14. A cyclist traveled at 24 miles per hour for 3 hours. How many total miles did he travel?

    A. 72

    B. 56

    C. 24

    D. 18

15. Denise has taken four math tests this semester and has received grades of 89, 85, 96, and 87. What is the minimum score that Denise needs to receive in order to get an average math grade of at least 90?

    A. 85

    B. 89

    C. 90

    D. 93

16. A car drove at 70 miles per hour for 3.5 hours. How far did it travel in total?

    A. 110 miles

    B. 245 miles

    C. 300 miles

    D. 325 miles

17. A gram of fat contains 9 calories. An 1,800-calorie diet allows no more than 30% of the calories from fat. How many grams of fat are allowed in the diet?

    A. 60

    B. 70

    C. 80

    D. 90

18. There are 150 students in math courses at Princeton High School. 73 are in geometry, 62 are in algebra, and 52 are in neither course. How many students are in both geometry and algebra?

A. 37

B. 47

C. 52

D. 59

19. The River Line charges $7.50 for tickets bought before 5:00 P.M. and $9.25 for tickets bought after 5:00 P.M. If 80 tickets were sold on a certain day for a total of $699.75, how many were sold after 5:00 P.M.?

A. 34

B. 57

C. 69

D. 72

20. Kathy put $1,500 down on a car that represents 8% of the total cost of the car. What is the total cost of the car?

A. $20,900

B. $18,750

C. $16,980

D. $14,230

21. John can run 6 miles per hour and Bill can run 4 miles per hour. If they run in opposite directions for 2 hours, then how far apart will they be?

A. 20

B. 12

C. 10

D. 8

22. John can bench press 400 pounds. Gene can bench press 300 pounds. How much more can John press than Gene?

    A. 50
    B. 100
    C. 300
    D. 400

23. Jim reads 1 page of a 28-page book the first night, 2 the second night, 3 the third night, and so on. How many days will it take him to finish the book?

    A. 4
    B. 5
    C. 6
    D. 7

24. The Air Force base has a soccer team with 7 privates and 17 sergeants on it. What is the ratio of the total number of players on the team to the number of sergeants on the team?

    A. 7:17
    B. 17:7
    C. 17:24
    D. 24:17

25. Jim earns $7.25 per hour. How much does he earn if he works 40 hours?

    A. $29.00
    B. $129.00
    C. $210.00
    D. $290.00

26. A store sells cheese for $4.00 for the first pound and $2.50 for each additional pound. How many pounds of cheese could be bought with $29.00?

    A. 9

    B. 10

    C. 11

    D. 12

27. A barracks now houses 40 recruits and allows 52 square feet of space per recruit. If 5 more recruits are placed in the barracks, to the nearest square root how much less space will each recruit get?

    A. 3 square feet

    B. 5 square feet

    C. 6 square feet

    D. 7 square feet

28. Supply Truck A left the base at 8:00 A.M. traveling on the highway at 40 miles per hour. At 11:00 A.M., Supply Truck B left the same base, traveling on the same road at 60 miles per hour. At what time did Supply Truck B catch up with Supply Truck A?

    A. 5:00 P.M.

    B. 4:00 P.M.

    C. 3:00 P.M.

    D. 2:00 P.M.

29. The following chart shows how many hours per day Airman Smith worked in the recruiting booth at the local mall. What is the average number of hours that she worked for the five days?

    A. 5.5

    B. 4.4

    C. 4.0

    D. 3.5

Monday	Tuesday	Wednesday	Thursday	Friday
5	4	8	0	5

30. One number is 5 times another number and their sum is 60. What is the lesser of the two numbers?

    A. 10

    B. 15

    C. 45

    D. 50

ANSWERS AND EXPLANATIONS

1. (C).

$$4.50 = \frac{3}{4}x$$
$$18.00 = 3x$$
$$6.00 = x$$

His total allowance was $6.00. This amount minus the cost of the movie leaves $1.50 for the week.

2. (A). Rate $= \dfrac{\text{distance}}{\text{time}}$

$$\frac{15 \text{ miles per hour}}{60 \text{ minutes}} = \frac{x \text{ miles}}{1 \text{ minute}}$$
$$\frac{15}{60} = \frac{x}{1}$$
$$\frac{60x}{60} = \frac{15}{60}$$
$$x = \frac{1}{4}$$

If it takes Kathy one minute to ride $\frac{1}{4}$ mile, it will take her 2 minutes to ride $\frac{1}{2}$ mile.

3. (B). The total number is the unknown, x. So, $\frac{7}{8}x = 14$.

$$7x = 8(14)$$
$$7x = 112$$
$$x = 16$$

4. (D).

$$\frac{2}{52} = \frac{10}{x}$$
$$2x = 52 \times 10$$
$$x = \frac{520}{2}$$
$$x = \$260$$

5. (D). 10% of \$24.00 is \$2.40.

$$\$24.00 - \$2.40 = \$21.60$$

6. (B). You need to convert the length to inches, so 3 feet 6 inches is 42 inches. 42 inches × the number of pieces of wood needed is $42 \times 4 = 168$.

$$\frac{168}{12} = 14$$

7. (C). Since 12 of the students in the class are girls and 60% of the students are boys, 100% − 60% = 40% (girls).

$$\text{Percent} \times \text{whole} = \text{part}$$
$$40\% \times \text{whole} = 12$$
$$.4 \times \text{whole} = 12$$
$$\text{Whole} = \frac{12}{.4}$$
$$\text{Whole} = 30$$

8. (C). $600 - 68 = 532$. Add $532 + 45 = 577$.

9. (A).

$$\frac{20}{500} = \frac{x}{25}$$
$$20(25) = 500x$$
$$500 = 500x$$
$$x = 1$$

10. (C).

$$\frac{8}{10} = \frac{x}{25}$$
$$(25)(8) = 10x$$
$$200 = 10x$$
$$x = 20$$

11. (C). Let x represent the total number of minutes on his plan. Since Cecil has $\frac{12}{25}$ of the minutes left, he has used $1 - \frac{12}{25} = \frac{13}{25}$ of the minutes, $\frac{13}{25x} = 260$ minutes.

$$\frac{13}{25x} = 260$$
$$13x = 25(260)$$
$$13x = 6{,}500$$
$$x = 500$$

12. (D). Regina had a total of $18 - 4 = 14$ vacation days she used $\left(\frac{1}{2}\right)(14) = 7$ days.

13. (D).

$$\text{Average} = \frac{128}{8}$$
$$A = 16$$

14. (A). $\dfrac{24 \text{ miles}}{\text{hour}} \times 3 \text{ hours} = 72 \text{ miles}$

15. (D).

$$90 = \frac{89 + 85 + 96 + 87 + x}{5}$$
$$90 = \left(\frac{357 + x}{5}\right)(5)$$
$$450 = 357 + x$$
$$450 - 357 = 357 - 357 + x$$
$$93 = x$$

16. (B).

$$\text{Rate} = \frac{\text{distance}}{\text{time}}$$

$$70 \text{ miles per hour} = \frac{x}{3.5}\text{hours}$$

$$70 \times 3.5 = \frac{x}{3.5} \times 3.5$$

$$x = 245 \text{ miles}$$

17. (A). 30% of 1,800, or .03 × 1800 = 540 calories allowed from fat. Since there are 9 calories in each gram of fat, $\frac{540}{9} = 60$.

18. (A). If 52 students are in neither class, then 98 are in algebra or geometry. The rest are 73 + 62 = 135 students. Since this number is greater than the 98 students in algebra or geometry, the difference between 135 and 98 is the number of students enrolled in both algebra and geometry: 135 − 98 = 37.

19. (B).

$$9.25x + 7.50(80-x) = 699.75$$
$$9.25x + 600 - 7.50x = 699.75$$
$$1.75x = 99.75$$
$$x = 57$$

20. (B).

$$\text{Percent} = \frac{\text{part}}{\text{whole}}$$

$$8\% \text{ or } .08 = \frac{1,500}{\text{total cost of car}}$$

$$0.08 \times \text{total cost of car} = \frac{1,500}{.08}$$

$$\text{Total cost of car} = \$18,750$$

21. (A). The rate they are moving away from each other is 4 + 6 miles per hour, or 10 miles per hour. In 2 hours this distance would be 20 miles.

22. (B) 400 pounds − 300 pounds = 100 pounds

23. (D). The sum of the pages read is 28. 1 + 2 + 3 + 4 + 5 + 6 + 7 = 28.

24. (D).

$$\frac{\text{Total players on the team}}{\text{sergeants}} = \frac{7 + 17}{17}$$

$$= \frac{24}{17}, \text{ or } 24{:}17$$

25. (D). $7.25 × 40 hours = $290.00

26. (C).

First pound = $4.00. So $29.00 − $4.00 = $25.00 left to buy the additional pounds of cheese.

$$\$25.00 = \$2.50x$$
$$10 = x$$

Total number of pounds of cheese = 11

27. (C).

$$40 × 52 \text{ sq. ft} = 2{,}080 \text{ sq. ft.}$$
$$\frac{2{,}080}{45} = 46.22 \text{ sq. ft.}$$

Then 52 − 46.22 = 5.78, which is closest to 6 square feet

28. (A).

$$40(T + 3) = 60T$$
$$40T + 120 = 60T$$
$$120 = 20T$$
$$6 = T$$

Supply Truck B traveled for 6 hours. Since Truck B left at 11:00 A.M., it caught up with Truck A at 5:00 P.M.

29. (B). Average $= \dfrac{\text{sum}}{\text{number}} = \dfrac{5 + 4 + 8 + 0 + 5}{5}$

$\dfrac{22 \text{ hours}}{5} = 4.4 \text{ hours.}$

30. (A). One number is 5 times another number, and their sum is 60. You could rewrite that sentence as two equations and solve:

$$x = 5y$$
$$x + y = 60$$

So $5y + y = 60$, $6y = 60$, and $y = 10$.

If $y = 10$, $x = 5y = 5(10) = 50$.

The lesser of the two numbers is 10.

What Job Do You Really Want?

YOUR CAREER OPTIONS

Your potential for success is not the only factor to keep in mind when considering career goals. It is important to discover your interests and apply them to your search for a future occupation. The ASVAB is designed to measure your potential—it is up to you to decide what to do with it. It is often the case that the more interested you are in a specific area, the more you'll enjoy learning and working in that field.

The military has hundreds of job opportunities. The following Military Occupation Specialties (MOS) will give you an idea of some of the positions available in the Armed Services. There are lots of occupations and this is your chance to browse through your options and pursue what interests you. The occupations are listed by group to allow you to learn something about each one. If an occupation interests you, discuss it with your school guidance counselor or your local Armed Forces recruiter. The jobs we describe here are as up-to-date as they can be at printing time, but if you are interested in occupations that don't appear here, please discuss them with you counselor or recruiter.

Test Tip

Rehearse the test in these ways:

1. *Take REA's full-length practice AFQT in this book and the practice ASVAB online.*

2. *Review the directions for all of the question types.*

3. *Picture (in your mind) that your test experience will be very successful—that's called Positive Thinking!*

4. *Remember—you are not alone. Recruits all across the country are about to take the AFQT, just like you.*

Air Force Enlisted Jobs	
Operations	1A - Aircrew Operations 1C - Command & Control Systems Operations 1N - Intelligence 1P - Aircrew Equipment 1T - Aircrew Protection 1S - Safety 1U - Unmanned Aerospace Systems 1W - Weather
Maintenance & Logistics	2A - Manned Aerospace Maintenance 2F - Fuels 2G - Logistics Plans 2M - Missile & Space Systems Maintenance 2P - Precision Measurement Equipment Laboratory 2R - Maintenance Management Systems 2S - Supply 2T - Transportation & Vehicle Maintenance 2W - Munitions & Weapons
Support	3D - Cyberspace Support 3H - Historian 3M - Services 3N - Public Affairs 3P - Security Forces (Military Police) 3E - Civil Engineering 3S - Mission Support 3U - Manpower 3V - Visual Information
Medical & Dental	4X - Medical 4Y - Dental

(Continued from previous page)

Air Force Enlisted Jobs	
Legal & Chaplain	5J - Paralegal 5R - Chaplain Assistant
Finance & Contracting	6C - Contracting 6F - Financial
Special Investigations	7S - Special Investigations (OSI)
Special Duty Assignments	Special Duty Assignments are usually jobs that a member performs temporarily, working outside of their normal AFSC. When the special duty tour is completed, members usually return to their primary AFSC (enlisted job). Examples would be recruiter, first sergeant, or military training instructor. 8X - Special Duty Identifiers 9X - Special Reporting Identifiers

Army Enlisted Jobs	
Infantry Branch	11B - Infantryman 11C - Indirect Fire Infantryman 11X - Infantryman (status upon infantry initial entry training; turns into 11B or 11C) 11Z - Infantry Senior Sergeant (Rank 1sgt) 11H - Infantry Anti-Armor Specialist (no longer a separate MOS; reclassified 11B) 11M - Mechanized Infantryman (no longer a separate MOS; reclassified 11B)

Continued →

(Continued from previous page)

Army Enlisted Jobs	
Field Artillery Branch	13B - Cannon Crewmember 13C - TAC Fire Operations Specialist 13D - Field Artillery Tactical Data Systems Specialist 13E - Cannon Fire Direction Specialist 13F - Fire Support Specialist 13M - Multiple Launch Rocket System Crewmember 13P - MLRS/LANCE Operations Fire Directions Specialist 13R - Field Artillery Fire Finder Radar Operator 13S - Field Artillery Surveyor 13W - Field Artillery Meteorological Crewmember 13X - Field Artillery Enlistment Option (turns into 13B, 13C, 13D, 13E, 13F, 13M, 13P, or 13R) 13Z - Field Artillery Senior Sergeant
Air Defense Artillery Branch	14E - Patriot Fire Control Enhanced Operator/ Maintainer 14J - Early Warning System Operator 14M - Man Portable Air Defense System Crewmember 14R - Bradley Linebacker Crewmember 14S - Avenger Crewmember 14T - PATRIOT Launching Station Enhanced Operator/Maintainer 14Z - Air Defense Artillery (ADA) Senior Sergeant
Aviation Branch	15B - Aircraft Power Plant Repairer 15D - Aircraft Power Train Repairer 15F - Aircraft Electrician 15G - Aircraft Structural Repairer

(Continued from previous page)

Army Enlisted Jobs	
Aviation Branch (*continued*)	15H - Aircraft Pneudraulic Repairer 15J - OH-58D Armament/Electrical/Avionics Systems Repairer 15K - Aircraft Components Repair Supervisor 15M - UH-1 Helicopter Repairer 15N - Avionics Mechanic 15P - Aviation Operations Specialist 15Q - Air Traffic Control Operator 15R - AH-64 Attack Helicopter Repairer 15S - OH-58D Helicopter Repairer 15T - UH-60 Helicopter Repairer 15U - Medium Helicopter Repairer 15V - Observation/Scout Helicopter Repairer 15X - AH-64 Armament/Electrical Systems Repairer 15Y - AH-64D Armament/ Electrical Systems Repairer 15Z - Aircraft Maintenance Senior Sergeant
Special Forces Branch	18B - Special Forces Weapons Sergeant 18C - Special Forces Engineer Sergeant 18D - Special Forces Medical Sergeant 18E - Special Forces Communications Sergeant 18F - Special Forces Assistant Operations & Intelligence Sergeant 18X - Special Forces Candidate 18Z - Special Forces Operations Sergeant
Armor Branch	19D - Cavalry Scout 19K - Armor Crewmember 19Z - Armor Senior Sergeant

Continued →

(Continued from previous page)

Army Enlisted Jobs	
Corps of Engineers Branch	21B - Combat Engineer (Formally 12B) 21C - Bridge Crewmember 21D - Diver 21E - Heavy Construction Equipment Operator 21G - Quarrying Specialist 21H - Construction Engineer 21J - General Construction Equipment Operator 21K - Plumber 21L - Lithographer 21M - Firefighter 21N - Construction Equipment Supervisor 21P - Prime Power Production Specialist 21Q - Transmission and Distribution Specialist 21R - Interior Electrician 21S - Topographic Surveyor 21T - Technical Engineering Specialist 21U - Topographic Analyst 21V - Concrete and Asphalt Equipment Operator 21W - Carpentry and Masonry Specialist 21X - General Engineering Supervisor 21Y - Topographic Engineering Supervisor 21Z - Combat Engineering Senior Sergeant
Signal Corps Branch	25B - Information Technology Specialist 25C - Radio Operator Maintainer 25F - Network Switching Systems Operator/ Maintainer 25L - Wire Systems Installer 25M - Multimedia Illustrator 25N - Nodal Network Systems Operator/Maintainer 25P - Microwave Systems Operator/Maintainer

(Continued from previous page)

Army Enlisted Jobs	

Signal Corps Branch (*continued*)	25Q - Multichannel Transmission Systems Operator
	25R - Visual Information/Audio Equipment Repairer
	25S - Satellite Communication Systems Operator/
	    Maintainer
	25T - Satellite/Microwave Systems Chief
	25U - Signal Support Systems Specialist
	25V - Combat Documentation & Production
	    Specialist
	25W - Telecommunications Operations Chief
	25X - Senior Signal Sergeant
	25Z - Visual Information Operations Chief

Judge Advocate General Branch	27D - Paralegal Specialist
Military Police Corps Branch	31B - Military Police 31D - CID Special Agent 31E - Internment/Resettlement Specialist
Military Intelligence Branch	33W (35T) - MI Systems Maintainer/Integrator 96B (35F) - Intelligence Analyst 96D (35G) - Imagery Analyst 96H (35H) - Imagery Ground Station Operator 96R (35H) - Ground Surveillance Systems Operator 96U (35K) - Unmanned Aerial Vehicle Operator 96Z (35X) - Intelligence Senior Sergeant 97B (35L) - Counterintelligence Agent 97E (35M) - Human Intelligence Collector 97L (35Q) - Translator/Interpreter 97Z (35Y) - Counterintelligence/Human Intelligence Senior Sergeant

Continued ➡

(Continued from previous page)

Army Enlisted Jobs	
Military Intelligence Branch (*continued*)	98C (35N) - Signal Intelligence Analyst (Linguist) 98G (35P) - Cryptologic Linguist 98P (35U) - Multi-Sensor Operator 98Y (35S) - Signals Collector/Analyst 98Z (35Z) - Signals Intelligence Senior Sergeant 09L (35V) - Translator Aide 05h EW/SIGINT - Morse Intercept Operator
Psychological Operations Corps Branch	37F Psychological Operations Specialist
Civil Affairs Branch	38B Civil Affairs Specialist
Adjutant General Branch	42A - Human Resource Specialist 42F - Human Resource Systems Information Specialist 42R9B - Trumpet Player 42R9C - Baritone or Euphonium Player 42R9D - French Horn Player 42R9E - Trombone Player 42R9F - Tuba Player 42R9G - Flute or Piccolo Player 42R9H - Oboe Player 42R9J - Clarinet Player 42R9K - Bassoon Player 42R9L - Saxophone Player 42R9M - Percussion Player 42R9N - Piano Player 42R9T - Guitar Player 42R9U - Electric Bass Guitar Player 42S - Special Band Member

(Continued from previous page)

Army Enlisted Jobs	
Finance Branch	44C Finance Specialist/Accounting Specialist
Public Affairs Branch	46Q Public Affairs Specialist 46R Broadcast Journalist 46Z Public Affairs Chief
Chaplain Branch	56M - Chaplain Assistant
CMF 63 - Mechanical Maintenance	44B - Metal Worker 44E - Machinist 45B - Small Arms/Artillery Repairer 45G - Fire Control Repairer 45K - Armament Repairer 52C - Utilities Equipment Repairer 52D - Power Generation Equipment Repairer 62B - Construction Equipment Repairer 63A - M1 Abrams Tank Turret Mechanic/M1 Abrams Tank System Mechanic 63B - Light-Wheel Vehicle Mechanic/Heavy-Wheel Vehicle Mechanic/Wheel Vehicle Repairer 63D - Artillery Mechanic 63H - Fuel and Electrical Repairer/Track Vehicle Mechanic 63J - Quartermaster and Chemical Equipment Repairer 63M - M2-3 Bradley Fighting Vehicle System Mechanic/Bradley Fighting Vehicle Systems Turret Mechanic 63X - Track Vehicle Repairer 63W - All-Wheel Vehicle Repairer 63Z - Mechanical Maintenance Supervisor

Continued ➞

(Continued from previous page)

Army Enlisted Jobs	
Medical Department Branches	68A - Medical Equipment Repairer 68D - Operating Room Specialist 68E - Dental Specialist 68G - Patient Administration Specialist 68H - Optical Laboratory Specialist 68J - Medical Logistic Specialist 68K - Medical Laboratory Specialist 68M - Hospital Food Specialist 68P - Radiology Specialist 68Q - Pharmacy Specialist 68R - Veterinary Food Inspection Specialist 68S - Preventive Medicine Specialist 68T - Animal Care Specialist 68V - Respiratory Specialist 68W - Health Care Specialist (aka Combat Medic) 68X - Mental Health Specialist 68Z - Chief Medical NCO
Chemical Branch	74D - Chemical Operations Specialist (formerly 54B)
CMF 79 - Recruiting and Retention	79R - Recruiter Noncommissioned Officer 79S - Career Counselor 79T - Recruiting and Retention NCO 79V - Retention and Transition Noncommissioned Officer
Transportation Branch	88H - Cargo Specialist 88K - Watercraft Operator 88L - Watercraft Engineer 88M - Motor Transport Operator

(Continued from previous page)

Army Enlisted Jobs	
Transportation Branch (*continued*)	88N - Traffic Management Coordinator 88P - Railway Equipment Repairer 88T - Railway Section Repairer 88U - Railway Operations Crewmember 88Z - Transportation Senior Sergeant
Ordnance Branch	89B - Ammunition Specialist 89D - Explosive Ordnance Disposal Specialist
Quartermaster Corps Branch	92A - Automated Logistical Specialist 92F - Petroleum Supply Specialist 92G - Food Service Specialist 92L - Petroleum Laboratory Specialist 92M - Mortuary Affairs Specialist 92R - Parachute Rigger 92S - Shower/Laundry and Clothing Repair Specialist 92W - Water Treatment Specialist 92Y - Unit Supply Specialist 92Z - Senior Noncommissioned Logistician
CMF 94 - Electronic Maintenance	94A - Land Combat Electronic Missile System Repairer 94D - Air Traffic Control Equipment Repairer 94E - Radio and Communications Security Repairer 94F - Special Electronics Devices Repairer 94H - Test, Measurement & Diagnostic Equipment Support Specialist 94K - Automatic Test Equipment Operator/ Maintainer 94L - Avionics Communications Equipment Repairer 94M - Radar Repairer

Continued ➝

(Continued from previous page)

Army Enlisted Jobs	
CMF 94 - Electronic Maintenance (*continued*)	94P - Multiple Launch Rocket System Repairer
	94R - Avionics System Repairer
	94S - PATRIOT System Repairer
	94T - Avenger System Repairer
	94W - Electronic Maintenance Chief
	94Y - Integrated Family of Test Equipment
	94Z - Senior Electronic Maintenance Chief

Marines Enlisted Jobs	
Personnel & Administration: Occupational Field 01	Administrative Clerk
	Unit Diary Clerk
	Personnel Clerk
	Postal Clerk
Intelligence: Occupational Field 02	Jobs include: signals intelligence, communications intelligence operator analyst, and cryptologic linguist.
	Intelligence Specialist
Infantry: Occupational Field 03	Rifleman
	Machine Gunner
	Mortar Man
	Assaultman
	Light Armored Vehicle Crewman
	Antitank Assault Missile

(Continued from previous page)

Marines Enlisted Jobs	
Logistics: Occupational Field 04	Logistics/Embarkation Specialist Maintenance Management Specialist Air Delivery Specialist Landing Support Specialist
Field Artillery: Occupational Field 08	Field Artillery Fire Controlman Field Artillery Meteorological Crewman Field Artillery Cannoneer Fire Support Man Field Artillery, Radar Operator
Utilities: Occupational Field 11	Refrigeration Mechanic Basic Hygiene Equipment Operator Basic Electrician Electrical Equipment Repair Specialist Fabric Repair Specialist
Engineer, Construction, Equipment & Shore Party: Occupational Field 13	Basic Combat Engineer Engineer Equipment Mechanic Basic Metal Worker Engineer Equipment Operator Engineer Assistant Bulk Field Specialist
Printing & Reproduction: Occupational Field 15	Lithographer

Continued →

(Continued from previous page)

Marines Enlisted Jobs	
Tank & Amphibian Tractor: Occupational Field 18	Tank Crewman Assault Amphibian Crewman
Ordnance: Occupational Field 21	Machinist Assault Amphibian Repairman Main Battle Tank Repairman Small Arms Repair Electro-Optical Instrument Repair Light Armored Vehicle Repair Towed Artillery System
Ammunition & Explosives Ordnance Disposal: Occupational Field 23	Ammunition Technician
Operational Communications: Occupational Field 23	ULCS Operational Maintainer Field Radio Operator Communications Center Operator Construction Wireman Ground MOB for SATCOM Terminal Operator High Frequency Communications Central Operator Multi-Channel Equipment Operator Field Wireman Fleet SATCOM Terminal Operator

(Continued from previous page)

Marines Enlisted Jobs	
Signal Intelligence/ Ground Electronic Warfare: Occupational Field 26	Basic Electronic Intelligence Operational Analysis
Data/Communications Maintenance: Occupational Field 28	Ground Radar Repair Radio Technician Telephone Technician Cable Systems Technician PC Tact Office Machine Technician Electronic Switching Equipment Technician Multi-Channel Equipment Repair Test Measures/Diagnostic Equipment Repair Communications Security Equipment Repair Artillery Electronic Systems Repair Counter Mortar Radar Repair
Supply Administrations & Operations: Occupational Field 30	Supply Administrations & Operations Clerk Basic Packing Specialist Warehouse Clerk
Transportation: Occupational Field 31	Jobs include: heavy vehicle operator, motor vehicle operator, and logistics vehicle systems operator. Traffic Management Specialist
Food Service: Occupational Field 33	Jobs include: food service specialist. Basic Food Service Specialist Subsistence Supply Clerk

Continued ➡

(Continued from previous page)

Marines Enlisted Jobs	
Auditing, Finance & Accounting: Occupational Field 34	Disbursing Technician Fiscal Budget Technician
Data Systems: Occupational Field 40	Automotive Organizational Maintenance Logistics Vehicle Operator Body Repair Mechanic Motor Vehicle Operator Vehicle Recovery Operator ADA Programming Small Computer Systems Specialist
Public Affairs: Occupational Field 43	Combat Correspondent Ft. Meade, MD
Legal Services: Occupational Field 44	Jobs include: administrative clerk, postal clerk, legal services specialist, aircraft maintenance administrative clerk, and aviation operations specialist. Legal Services Specialist
Training & Audio-Visual Support: Occupational Field 46	Jobs include: graphics specialist, combat photographic specialist, and combat motion media photographer. Combat Visual Information Equipment Specialist Graphics Specialist Combat Photographic Specialist Combat/Motion Media Specialist

(Continued from previous page)

Marines Enlisted Jobs	
Band: Occupational Field 55	Drum & Bugle Corps Music, Basic Music, Intermediate Music, Assistant Bandleader
Nuclear, Biological & Chemical (NBC): Occupational Field 57	NBC Defense Specialist
Military Police & Corrections: Occupational Field 58	Jobs include: military police and correctional specialist. Law Enforcement (Military Police)
Electronics Maintenance: Occupational Field 59	Jobs include: aviation radar repair, aircraft electrical systems technician, weapon system specialist, camera systems technician, and aircraft cryptographic systems technician. Aviation Radio Repairer Tactical Air Operations Central Technician Tactical Data Communications Central Technician Tactical Air Command Central Repairer Tactical Data Communications Central Repairer Aviation Radar Repairer
Electronics Maintenance: Occupational Field 59	Air Traffic Control Unit Navigational Aids Technician Air Traffic Control Unit Communications Technician Air Traffic Control Unit Radar Technician

Continued ➜

(Continued from previous page)

Marines Enlisted Jobs	
Electronics Maintenance: Occupational Field 59 (*continued*)	Air Traffic Control Unit Navigational Aids Repair
	Air Traffic Control Unit Radar Repairer
	Air Traffic Control Unit Communications Repairer
	Data Systems Technician
	Tactical General Purpose Computer
Aircraft Maintenance: Occupational Field 60/61	Jobs include: aircraft or helicopter power plant mechanic, aircraft safety equipment mechanic, and aircraft or helicopter airframe mechanic.
	Aviation Maintenance Administration
	Aviation Safety Equipment Mechanic
	Cryogenics Equipment Operators
	Aircraft Mechanic KC-130
	Aircraft Mechanic F/A-18
	Aircraft Power Plants Mechanic
	KC-130 Aircraft Flight Mechanic
	Aircraft Hydraulic Airframe Mechanic
	Aircraft Structure Airframe Mechanic
	Flight Equipment
	Aircraft Maintenance GSE M/R
	Aircraft Intermediate Level Structure Mechanic
	Aircraft Intermediate Level Hydraulic/ Pneumatic Mechanic
	Helicopter Mechanic
	Helicopter Power Plant Mechanical Technician
	Helicopter Power Plant Mechanic

(Continued from previous page)

Marines Enlisted Jobs	
Aircraft Maintenance: Occupational Field 60/61 (*continued*)	Helicopter Dynamic Comp Mechanic
	Helicopter Hydraulic/Pneumatic Mechanic
	Helicopter Structure Mechanic
	Helicopter Structure Mechanic U/AH
	CH-46 Crew Chief
	CH-53 Crew Chief
	UH-1N Crew Chief
Avionics: Occupational Field 63/64	A/C Comm/Nav Radar Systems
	A/C Comm/Nav/Wpns Systems
	A/C Comm/Nav/Wpns
	A/C Comm/Nav Electronics
	A/C Elec Sys Tech KC
	A/C Elec/Sys Tech F
	A/C EleCntrmrs Systems
	A/C Comm/Nav Sys Technician
	A/C Nav Sys Tech IFF
	Aviation Elec Micro-Miniature
	A/C Elec/Inst Flight Counter
	A/CFlt Tech Helo/OV
	Aviation Test Set Tech IMA
	Radar Test Stat/Rad
	A/C Internal Nav Systems
	Hybrid Test Set Technician
	A/C Fwd Looking Rad
	Consol Auto Sup Systems

Continued →

(Continued from previous page)

Marines Enlisted Jobs	
Avionics: Occupational Field 63/64 (*continued*)	A/C Elec Equipment Tester
	A/C Elec Counter Systems
	Aviation Precision Measurement
	Aviation Meteorological Electronics
	Computer Sys Tech DP
Aviation Ordnance: Occupational Field 65	Aviation Ordnance Ammo Technician
	Aviation Ordnance Equipment Repairman
	Aircraft Ordnance Technician
Aviation Supply: Occupational Field 66	Aviation Supply Clerk
	Auto Information Systems Computer Operator
Weather Service: Occupational Field 68	Weather Observer
Airfield Services: Occupational Field 70	Aviation Operations Specialist
	Aircraft Recovery Specialist
	Aircraft Firefighting/Rescue
Air Traffic Control/Air Control/Air Support/ Anti-Air Warfare: Occupational Field 72	Air Control Electronics
	Air Support Operations Operator
	Air Traffic Controller
	HAWK Missile Systems Operator
	LAAD Gunner
Enlisted Flight Crews: Occupational Field 73	First Navigator
	Airborne Radio Operator

Navy Enlisted Jobs
The Navy calls their enlisted jobs "ratings." Similar ratings are placed into various "communities."

Aviation Community	ABE - Aviation Boatswain's Mate - Launch/Recovery ABF - Aviation Boatswain's Mate - Fuels ABH - Aviation Boatswain's Mate - Aircraft Handler AC - Air Traffic Controller AD - Aviation Machinist's Mate AE - Aviation Electrician's Mate AG - Aerographer's Mate (Weather and Oceanography) AM - Aviation Structural Mechanic AME - Aviation Structural Mechanic - Safety Equipment AO - Aviation Ordnanceman AS - Aviation Support Equipment Technician AT - Aviation Electronics Technician AW - Aviation Warfare Systems Operator AZ - Aviation Maintenance Administrationman PR - Aircrew Survival Equipmentman
Cryptologic Community (Language and Computers).	CTI - Cryptologic Technician - Interpretive CTM - Cryptologic Technician - Maintenance CTN - Cryptologic Technician - Networks CTR - Cryptologic Technician - Collection CTT - Cryptologic Technician - Technical IT - Information System Technician
Intelligence Community	IS - Intelligence Specialist

Continued ➡

(Continued from previous page)

Navy Enlisted Jobs	
Medical/Dental Community	HM - Hospital Corpsman
Nuclear Community	NF - Nuclear Field Enlistment Program EM(N) - Nuclear Trained Electrician's Mate ET(N) - Nuclear Trained Electronics Technician MM(N) - Nuclear Trained Machinist's Mate
SEABEE Community (Construction)	BU - Builder CE - Construction Electrician CM - Construction Mechanic EA - Engineering Aid EO - Equipment Operator SW - Steelworker UT - Utilitiesman
Security Community	MA - Master at Arms
Special Warfare/ Special Operations Community	EOD - Explosive Ordnance Disposal ND - Navy Diver SO - Special Operations (Navy SEAL) SB - Special Warfare Boat Operator
Submarine Community	CS(SS) - Culinary Specialist (Submarine) ET COM - Electronics Technician (Communications) ET NAV - Electronics Technician (Navigation) FT - Fire Control Technician MM AUX - Machinist Mate (Auxiliary Equipment) MM WEP - Machinist Mate (Weapons) MT - Missile Technician

(Continued from previous page)

Navy Enlisted Jobs	
Submarine Community (***continued***)	SK(SS) - Storekeeper (Submarine) STS - Sonar Technician (Submarine) YN(SS) - Yeoman (Submarine)
Supply Community	CS - Culinary Specialist LS - Logistic Support (effective Oct 2009) SH - Ship's Serviceman
Surface Combat Systems/ Operations Community	BM - Boatswain's Mate ET - Electronic Technician FC - Fire Controlman GM - Gunner's Mate MN - Mineman OS - Operations Specialist QM - Quartermaster STG - Sonar Technician - Surface
Surface Engineering Community	DC - Damage Controlman EM - Electricians Mate EN - Engineman GSE - Gas Turbine Systems Technician - Electrical GSM - Gas Turbine Systems Technician - Mechanical HT - Hull Maintenance Technician IC - Interior Communications Electrician MM - Machinist's Mate MR - Machinery Repairman

AFQT Practice Test

Practice AFQT

Part 1: Word Knowledge

Part 2: Paragraph Comprehension

Part 3: Mathematics Knowledge

Part 4: Arithmetic Reasoning

This Practice Test contains the four sections of the Armed Services Vocational Aptitude Battery that account for the Armed Forces Qualifying Test.

To experience a complete ASVAB practice test, go to *www.rea.com/asvab.*

PART 1

Word Knowledge

Time: 11 Minutes
35 Questions

---------------- **DIRECTIONS** ----------------

This test is a test of your vocabulary. Each question has an underlined word. You may be asked to choose which of the four choices most nearly means the same thing as the word that is underlined or you may be asked which of the four choices means the opposite. If the word in the sentence is underlined, then select the answer choice that most nearly means the word that is underlined. On your answer sheet, mark the space that matches your choice. Be sure you are marking your answer in the space that represents the proper question number.

---

1. The best synonym for <u>persuade</u> is
   A. convince.
   B. believe.
   C. sweat.
   D. permeate.

2. The best synonym for <u>conversion</u> is
   A. talk.
   B. transformation.
   C. come together.
   D. revelation.

3. The best synonym for
   <u>chagrin</u> is
   A. horror.
   B. boredom.
   C. grief.
   D. distress.

4. The best synonym for <u>resist</u> is
   A. save.
   B. turn off.
   C. live.
   D. oppose.

5. Sandy believed most teenage
   girls were <u>superficial</u> because
   of their preoccupation with
   shopping.
   A. shallow
   B. excessive
   C. flighty
   D. important

6. The best synonym for
   <u>obsolete</u> is
   A. inconvenient.
   B. discontinued.
   C. unrewarding.
   D. futile.

7. The best synonym for <u>fitful</u> is
   A. irregular.
   B. sound.
   C. jaunty.
   D. undisciplined.

8. The best synonym for
   <u>humble</u> is
   A. delicious.
   B. arrogant.
   C. tedious.
   D. modest.

9. Every five years the rules of
   the league were reviewed
   and <u>modified</u> if necessary.
   A. limited
   B. obscured
   C. altered
   D. updated

10. The best synonym for <u>scold</u> is
    A. confuse.
    B. berate.
    C. weaken.
    D. flatter.

11. The best synonym for
    <u>evade</u> is
    A. intrude.
    B. elude.
    C. abandon.
    D. disappear.

12. The best synonym for
    <u>deceive</u> is
    A. get.
    B. mislead.
    C. promise.
    D. create.

13. The secretary had an <u>urgent</u> message to deliver to the company president.
    A. tempting
    B. unnecessary
    C. professional
    D. important

14. The best synonym for <u>temper</u> is
    A. pace.
    B. lure.
    C. moderate.
    D. feud.

15. George's <u>fastidious</u> temperament soon drove his roommate crazy.
    A. rapid-paced
    B. demanding
    C. neat
    D. quirky

16. The best synonym for <u>appeal</u> is
    A. interest.
    B. be visible.
    C. calm.
    D. repel.

17. The best synonym for <u>virtuoso</u> is
    A. scholarly.
    B. skillful.
    C. kindly.
    D. passionate.

18. The best synonym for <u>inadvertent</u> is
    A. intentional.
    B. fickle.
    C. thoughtless.
    D. whimsical.

19. The best synonym for <u>profess</u> is
    A. affirm.
    B. teach.
    C. work.
    D. outline.

20. The best synonym for <u>reconcile</u> is
    A. settle.
    B. praise.
    C. memorize.
    D. rest.

21. The crook had been charged several times with being a <u>fraud</u>.
    A. vandal
    B. embezzler
    C. imposter
    D. thief

22. Would you care to <u>articulate</u> what you think the problem is?
    A. solve
    B. debate
    C. communicate
    D. consider

23. The best synonym for <u>clever</u> is
    A. knife-like.
    B. talented.
    C. dishonest.
    D. shrewd.

24. The best synonym for <u>disprove</u> is
    A. lie.
    B. deny.
    C. argue.
    D. prohibit.

25. The best synonym for <u>mediocre</u> is
    A. unsuccessful.
    B. healthy.
    C. imperfect.
    D. offensive.

26. The best synonym for <u>dismal</u> is
    A. spirited.
    B. depressing.
    C. frightening.
    D. weary.

27. The real estate agent said that $185,000 was <u>undoubtedly</u> the best offer the seller could expect.
    A. improbably
    B. generally
    C. impossibly
    D. certainly

28. The two girls had been <u>rivals</u> for almost their entire lives.
    A. colleagues
    B. servants
    C. employers
    D. competitors

29. The best synonym for <u>discriminate</u> is
    A. persecute.
    B. implicate.
    C. separate.
    D. doubt.

30. The best synonym for <u>introspection</u> is
    A. self-examination.
    B. shyness.
    C. concentration.
    D. quietness.

31. Characters in soap operas often experience <u>amnesia</u>.
    A. depression
    B. sleeplessness
    C. forgetfulness
    D. phobia

32. The best synonym for <u>ignorant</u> is
    A. inferior.
    B. disgraceful.
    C. inexperienced.
    D. foolish.

33. The best synonym for <u>covet</u> is

    A. shelter.

    B. steal.

    C. promise.

    D. desire.

34. The best synonym for <u>chronic</u> is

    A. repeat.

    B. painful.

    C. acute.

    D. brief.

35. The best synonym for <u>deference</u> is

    A. avoidance.

    B. dissimilarity.

    C. resistance.

    D. respect.

END OF PART 1. GO ON TO NEXT SECTION.➔

PART 2

Paragraph Comprehension

Time: 13 Minutes
15 Questions

_____ **DIRECTIONS** _____

This test consists of 15 paragraphs that test your ability to understand and retrieve information from passages you have read.
Each paragraph is followed by an incomplete question or statement. You must read each of the paragraphs and select the one
lettered choice that best completes the statement or question.

1. In the beginning, honey was mostly an article of local trade. Many
   farmers and villagers kept a few colonies of bees in box hives to
   supply their own needs and those of some friends, relatives, and
   neighbors. Moses Quimby of New York state was the first commercial
   beekeeper in the United States. As the use of improved hives and new
   honey-gathering methods became more widespread, commercial
   beekeeping spread to other states.

   The best title for this passage would be

   A. "A History of Beekeeping."
   B. "The Development of Commercial Beekeeping."
   C. "Moses Quimby—Commercial Beekeeper."
   D. "Beekeeping in New York State."

2. Alzheimer's disease includes serious forgetfulness—particularly about recent events—and confusion. At first the individual experiences only minor symptoms that people mistake for emotional upsets and other physical illnesses. Gradually, the victim becomes more forgetful. The affected person may neglect to turn off the oven, may misplace things, or may repeat already answered questions.

This passage does *not* imply that victims of Alzheimer's disease may

A. not remember childhood events.

B. suffer a gradual worsening of learning abilities.

C. forget recent events.

D. dislike particular foods.

3. Someone with a great desire to learn is said to be highly motivated. Motivation is very important in what one learns and how quickly one learns it. A motivated person will generally learn faster and more efficiently than an unmotivated one. To learn efficiently a person must *intend* to learn.

According to the passage, in order to learn quickly one must be

A. highly motivated.

B. unmotivated.

C. tired of learning.

D. in need of learning.

4. High tides arise on the sides of the Earth nearest to and farthest from the moon. At times of new moon and full moon, the sun's attraction reinforces that of the moon, producing higher (spring) tides. Halfway between new and full moon, solar attraction does not occur together with lunar attraction and therefore the difference between high and low tides is less; these lesser tides are called neap tides.

"Tides" are

A. the lowest level of water.

B. the rise and fall of bodies of water.

C. sea-level measurements.

D. the difference between the sun and the moon.

5. Isaac Newton's supreme scientific work was his theory of universal gravitation. He went to a farm in 1665 to avoid the plague, and during this time he worked out the law of gravity and its consequences for the solar system.

   According to the passage, the system of universal gravitation is Newton's

   A. least important scientific work.
   B. most disputed scientific work.
   C. most misunderstood scientific work.
   D. most important scientific work.

6. At present we are forced to look to other bodies in the solar system for hints as to what the early history of the Earth was like. Studies of our moon, Mercury, Mars, and the large satellites of Jupiter and Saturn have provided much evidence that all these large celestial bodies were bombarded by smaller objects shortly after the large bodies had formed.

   Which of the following bodies was *not* studied to give evidence that the Earth was bombarded in its early history?

   A. Mars
   B. Mercury
   C. Jupiter
   D. Earth's moon

7. Solar energy is becoming a logical alternative source of heat as the cost and unavailability of conventional fuels increases. Technology has now made the cost of harnessing the sun more economically possible. Solar heating and solar cooling are good for the environment, providing another reason to switch from conventional fuels.

   Solar heat is becoming a logical source of energy because conventional fuels are

   A. not expensive enough.
   B. becoming unavailable.
   C. attractive environmentally.
   D. are not as close as the sun.

8. Juan Ponce de Leon was the first Spaniard to touch the shores of the present-day United States. He never dreamed that his "island" of Florida was a peninsular extension of the vast North American continent. After coming to the New World, he led the occupation of Puerto Rico in 1508 and governed it from 1509 to 1512.

From the passage, the reader can assume that a "peninsula" is

A. a volcanic island.

B. an island completely surrounded by water.

C. an extension of land surrounded almost completely by water.

D. an island inhabited by Indians.

9. Horse owners who plan to breed one or more mares should know about heredity and know how to care for breeding animals and foals. The number of mares bred that actually conceive varies from about 40 to 85 percent, with the average running less than 50 percent. Some mares that do conceive fail to produce living foals.

To conceive is to

A. become sick.

B. become pregnant.

C. die.

D. be born.

10. Animals that produce large amounts of offspring depend upon the sheer size of the litter for the continuance of their species. The young mature very quickly, and are not educated, as the parents are usually involved with obtaining their own food and with reproduction. Should some of the offspring become endangered, the parents will not interfere.

Why would an animal parent *not* be able to care for its litter?

A. It is busy reproducing and gathering food.

B. It is busy educating the litter.

C. It interferes with the litter.

D. It is busy playing.

11. Phobic reactions are strong fears of specific objects or situations. For example, when a person is extremely fearful of birds, snakes, heights, or closed places when no danger exists, the label phobia is applied to the person's fear and avoidance. A person suffering from a phobia knows what he is afraid of and usually recognizes that his fear is irrational, but cannot control it.

    A phobia is a label for

    A. a person's ability to control fear.

    B. a person's fear and avoidance.

    C. a person's love of fear.

    D. a person's dislike of fear.

12. Asbestos millboard in wall and floor protection is a controversial issue because of the health hazard of asbestos fibers in the manufacturing, preparation, and handling of the millboard. The National Fire Protection Association is beginning to remove asbestos as a standard protection from fire. We strongly encourage the use of an alternative protection whenever one is available.

    The *overall* implication of the passage is

    A. asbestos is as safe as other building materials.

    B. only touching the asbestos fibers with your hands is harmful.

    C. asbestos can be harmful to one's health.

    D. using asbestos in building materials is fine.

13. From the dawn of civilization, the gaze of humanity has been drawn to the stars. The stars have been relied upon to direct travelers, to make agricultural predictions, to win wars, and to awaken love in the hearts of men and women. Ancient stargazers looking at the nighttime sky saw patterns emerge.

    This passage states that

    A. man never depends on the stars.

    B. stars are only for beautifying the skies.

    C. man has depended on stars at times.

    D. moons are the same as stars.

14. Try to make the visitor center your first stop at any park. There you will find information on attractions, activities, trails, and campsites. Descriptive films, literature, and exhibits will acquaint you with the geology, history, and plant and animal life of the area.

   The background material described includes all of the following *except*

   A. interviews with inhabitants.
   B. exhibits.
   C. literature.
   D. films.

15. The most popular organic gem is the pearl. A pearl occurs when a marine mollusk reacts to an irritating impurity accidentally introduced into its body. A *cultured* pearl is the result of the intentional insertion of a mother-of-pearl bead into a live mollusk. Either way, the pearl-making process is the same: The mollusk covers the irritant with a substance called nacre.

   Nacre is a substance that is

   A. mechanically manufactured.
   B. the result of laboratory testing.
   C. organically secreted by the mollusk.
   D. present in the chemicals of freshwater ponds.

END OF PART 2. GO ON TO NEXT SECTION.→

PART 3

Mathematics Knowledge

Time: 24 Minutes
25 Questions

---------------- **DIRECTIONS** ----------------

Each question has four multiple-choice answers, labeled by the number of the question and the letters A, B, C or D. Select the single answer which is correct.

---

1. If one angle of a right triangle is 70°, then how many degrees are there in the smallest angle?

   A. 20°

   B. 25°

   C. 30°

   D. 35°

2. What is the square root of 196?

   A. 11

   B. 12

   C. 13

   D. 14

3. If $-6x > -12$, then which of the following must be true?

   A. $x > 2$

   B. $x \geq 2$

   C. $x < 2$

   D. $x \leq 2$

4. If the perimeter of a square equals one foot, then what is the area of this square (in square inches)?

   A. 7

   B. 8

   C. 9

   D. 10

5. What does $(x - 2)(x - 3)$ equal?

   A. $x^2 + 5x - 6$

   B. $x^2 - 5x - 6$

   C. $x^2 + 5x + 6$

   D. $x^2 - 5x + 6$

6. If the length of a rectangle is twice the width and the perimeter equals 24, what would the equation look like assuming width equals w?

   A. $2w = 24$

   B. $3w = 24$

   C. $4w = 24$

   D. $6w = 24$

7. There are 200 girls in the freshman class. This is 40% of the freshman class. How many freshmen are there?

   A. 300

   B. 500

   C. 700

   D. 900

8. If $-10x \geq 65$, then which of the following must be true?

   A. $x < -6.5$

   B. $x \leq -6.5$

   C. $x > -6.5$

   D. $x \geq -6.5$

9. If one side of a right triangle equals one-half a foot and the hypotenuse equals ten inches, then what is the length of the other leg (in inches)?

   A. 8

   B. 9

   C. 10

   D. 11

10. If $9y - 26 = -8$, what is y?

    A. 5

    B. 4

    C. 3

    D. 2

11. What does $(z + 4)(z - 5)$ equal?

    A. $z^2 - 9z - 20$

    B. $z^2 + 9z - 20$

    C. $z^2 - z - 20$

    D. $z^2 - z + 20$

12. How many sides does a pentagon have?

    A. 4

    B. 5

    C. 6

    D. 7

13. If 60 people like to play basketball and 25% of them also play volleyball, how many play only basketball?

  A. 15

  B. 25

  C. 35

  D. 45

14. If a circle's area is equal to twice its circumference, what is the radius?

  A. 4

  B. 5

  C. 6

  D. 7

15. If $-x/3 > 4$, then which of the following must be true?

  A. $x < 12$

  B. $x < -12$

  C. $x > 12$

  D. $x > -12$

16. Factor $v^2 - 2v - 15$.

  A. $(v - 3)(v + 5)$

  B. $(v - 3)(v - 5)$

  C. $(v + 3)(v + 5)$

  D. $(v + 3)(v - 5)$

17. If a square having side s has the same perimeter as a rectangle with one side equal to four, what is the equation to find the other side, l, of the rectangle?

  A. $4s = 8 + 2l$

  B. $s = 4 + l$

  C. $4s = 4 + 3l$

  D. $4s = 8 + l$

18. If Jane reads ten pages each night for five nights, she will have 40% of her assignment done. How many pages does she have to read for her class?

  A. 100

  B. 125

  C. 150

  D. 175

19. If a right triangle has one angle equal to 25°, what is the difference in the angles formed by the hypotenuse?

  A. 25°

  B. 40°

  C. 65°

  D. 90°

20. What is the product of
   $(w + 6) (w + 2)$?

   A. $w^2 + 4w + 12$

   B. $w^2 + 6w + 12$

   C. $w^2 + 8w + 12$

   D. $w^2 - 8w + 12$

21. If a retailer wants to sell an
   item at 45% profit, how much
   must a $1.20 item sell for?

   A. $0.54

   B. $0.66

   C. $1.65

   D. $1.74

22. How many equal angles are
   there in an isosceles triangle?

   A. 0

   B. 2

   C. 3

   D. 4

23. What is the square root of
   169?

   A. 11

   B. 12

   C. 13

   D. 14

24. If $4x + 12 = 24$, then what
   is x?

   A. 3

   B. 4

   C. 5

   D. 6

25. If the area of a square is equal
   to twice its perimeter, what is
   the length of a side, s?

   A. 2

   B. 4

   C. 6

   D. 8

END OF PART 3. GO ON TO NEXT SECTION.→

PART 4

Arithmetic Reasoning

Time: 36 Minutes
30 Questions

DIRECTIONS

Each question has four multiple-choice answers, labeled by the number of the question and the letters A, B, C, or D. Select the single best answer.

1. Bill buys seven bags of chips for a party. Each bag costs $0.89. What is the total cost?

   A. $5.23

   B. $6.32

   C. $6.23

   D. $6.30

2. Scott earns $35,000 per year, and pays 28% tax. How much does he pay in tax per year?

   A. $10,500

   B. $10,000

   C. $9,000

   D. $9,800

3. A lion runs 50 miles per hour in pursuit of a zebra running at 40 miles per hour. If the initial distance between them was a quarter of a mile, how long will it take for the lion to catch the zebra?

   A. 1.5 minutes

   B. 1 minute

   C. 2 minutes

   D. 1.5 hours

4. Jeff opens a savings account (paying 5% interest) with $1,000 and a CD (paying 6% interest) with $2,000. After one year, how much interest does he earn?

   A. $17
   B. $50
   C. $120
   D. $170

5. A family bought a house for $120,000 and sold it two years later for $155,000. How much profit did they make?

   A. $30,000
   B. $35,000
   C. $40,000
   D. $50,000

6. A company had 500 employees. It laid off 68 of them, then hired back 43 of those. How many employees does the company now have?

   A. 475
   B. 432
   C. 543
   D. 568

7. An omelette requires three eggs. Six people meet for breakfast. How many eggs would be required if they all wanted omelettes?

   A. 16
   B. 17
   C. 18
   D. 19

8. A family of four has 12 rolls to serve as part of dinner. How many rolls will each person receive?

   A. 1
   B. 2
   C. 4
   D. 3

9. An athlete runs two miles in 13.5 minutes. How many minutes is this per mile?

   A. 6.5 minutes
   B. 6.75 minutes
   C. 7 minutes
   D. 7.5 minutes

10. Tracy has a 160-mile drive. She leaves at 8:00 and drives at 40 miles per hour. When will she arrive?

    A. 12:00
    B. 11:00
    C. 11:30
    D. 12:30

11. A running back averages 8.5 yards per carry in a football game. If he rushed for 136 yards in the game, then how many times did he carry the ball?

    A. 14
    B. 15
    C. 16
    D. 17

12. Twelve people go to a dance. Half of them are females, and half of the females are wearing black. How many females are wearing black?

    A. 4
    B. 1
    C. 2
    D. 3

13. Sandy earns $12 per hour. If she works overtime she earns time and a half. How much would she earn for two hours of overtime?

    A. $24
    B. $36
    C. $18
    D. $12

14. Marie's car gets 30 miles to the gallon of gas. If gas costs $1.29 per gallon and Marie wants to drive 20 miles, how much will this cost in gas?

    A. $0.86
    B. $2.58
    C. $25.80
    D. $38.70

15. Jimmy has $7 and spends $3.58 for lunch. How much does he have left?

    A. $3.58
    B. $3.40
    C. $3.42
    D. $3.50

16. Sam has to read 21 pages for homework in history, 16 pages in English, and 13 pages in math. How many pages must Sam read?

    A. 29
    B. 34
    C. 37
    D. 50

17. In a soccer league the record for most goals in a season is 21. Brian has already scored 17, and there are two games left. How many goals must he average per game to tie the record?

    A. 1
    B. 2
    C. 3
    D. 4

18. Grace has six skirts and four blouses. If she mixes and matches, how many combinations can she come up with?

    A. 24
    B. 10
    C. 15
    D. 20

19. If there are 24 hours in a day and seven days in a week, then how many hours are there in a week?

    A. 152
    B. 160
    C. 168
    D. 240

20. A boat usually goes 20 miles per hour, but now there is a wind of five miles per hour working against it. How long will it take this boat to travel 30 miles?

    A. 2 hours
    B. 1.5 hours
    C. 3 hours
    D. 2.5 hours

21. Each soccer team in a league has four defenders, but the all-star team will only have three defenders. If there are 16 teams, then how many defenders will not make the all-star team?

    A. 3
    B. 60
    C. 61
    D. 64

22. A grocer buys candy for 10¢ per package, then marks it up by 100% and then charges 10% tax. What is the final cost?

    A. 19¢
    B. 20¢
    C. 21¢
    D. 22¢

23. A towel manufacturer sells sets which consist of two towels and three washcloths. If he has 24 towels and 31 washcloths, how many sets can he sell?

A. 9

B. 10

C. 11

D. 12

24. Jackie comes to work at 8:30 AM, takes 45 minutes for lunch, and leaves at 5:15 PM. How long did she work?

A. 8 hours

B. 7.5 hours

C. 8.5 hours

D. 9 hours

25. On a winter morning it is −24 degrees in Detroit and 68 degrees in Los Angeles. How much colder is Detroit than Los Angeles?

A. 44 degrees

B. 24 degrees

C. 92 degrees

D. 68 degrees

26. In a school there are twice as many seniors as freshmen, and each class is half male and half female. If there are 300 male freshmen, then how many female seniors are there?

A. 900

B. 300

C. 1,200

D. 600

27. Mel does 80 push-ups every day for a week. How many did he do in that week?

A. 80

B. 160

C. 560

D. 800

28. A quarterback throws 30 passes in a game and completes 60%. How many were incomplete?

A. 12

B. 15

C. 18

D. 20

29. A company has 74 pads of paper in stock. The Accounting Department takes 16 pads, the Finance Department takes 12, and Research & Development takes 29. How many pads are left?

   A. 29

   B. 33

   C. 17

   D. 46

30. An independent auditor monitors the outgoing phone calls of employees in a small firm during a one-week period. One particular employee is on the phone for 24 minutes on Monday, 21 minutes on Tuesday, 13 minutes on Wednesday, 17 minutes on Thursday, and 15 minutes on Friday. What is this employee's average daily time on the phone?

   A. 16 minutes

   B. 17 minutes

   C. 18 minutes

   D. 19 minutes

END OF PRACTICE TEST.

Answers & Explanations

PART 1: WORD KNOWLEDGE ANSWER KEY

1. A	13. D	25. C
2. B	14. C	26. B
3. D	15. B	27. D
4. D	16. A	28. D
5. A	17. B	29. C
6. B	18. C	30. A
7. A	19. A	31. C
8. D	20. A	32. C
9. C	21. C	33. D
10. B	22. C	34. A
11. B	23. D	35. D
12. B	24. B	

DETAILED ANSWER EXPLANATIONS

1. **A** *Persuade* means convince. (B) *Believe,* meaning to think, to trust, or to have faith in, is not related. (C) *Sweat* is synonymous with perspire; (D) *permeate* is synonymous with pervade.

2. **B** *Conversion* most closely means a transformation. (A) *Talk* is synonymous with conversation; (C) *come together* is synonymous with convergence; (D) *revelation* is synonymous with enlightenment.

3. **D** *Chagrin* is distress caused by disappointment. (A) *Horror* is extreme fear, dismay, or dread; (B) *boredom* is restlessness or uninterestedness; (C) *grief* is a deep distress, a disaster, or an annoyance.

4. **D** *Resist* means to oppose. (A) *Save* can be synonymous with reserve; (B) *turn off* can mean to dismiss, evade, sell, accomplish, bore, deviate, or withdraw—but none of these has the same meaning as resist or oppose. (C) *Live* is synonymous with exist.

5. **A** *Superficial* means shallow or external, having to do only with the surface. (B) *Excessive* is synonymous with superfluous. (C) *Flighty* means frivolous or silly. (D) *Important* is an antonym of superficial.

6. **B** *Obsolete* means discontinued or outmoded. (A) *Inconvenient* is not related; (C) *unrewarding* means not valuable or satisfying; (D) *futile* means serving no useful purpose or frivolous.

7. **A** *Fitful* means irregular. When someone has had a fitful night's sleep, he has not slept well. (B) *Sound* is the opposite of fitful in the context of sleeping; and (C) *jaunty* and (D) *undisciplined* do not have similar meanings.

8. **D** *Humble* and *modest* both mean unpretentious or not proud. (A) To "eat humble pie" means to apologize or retract something previously said—but *humble* does not mean delicious! (B) *Arrogant*, to put oneself above others or be full of self-importance, is the opposite of humble; (C) *tedious* is synonymous with humdrum.

9. **C** *Modifed* means changed or altered. (A) *Limited* means restricted; (B) *obscured* means hidden or unclear; (D) *updated* is synonymous with modernized. *Modified may* mean updated, but it *always* means changed, so *altered* is the best synonym.

10. **B** *Scold* and *berate* both mean to find fault or rebuke. (A) *Confuse*, (C) *weaken*, and (D) *flatter* (praise excessively) have altogether different meanings.

11. **B** *Evade* and *elude* both mean to avoid. (A) *Intrude* means to invade; (C) *abandon* can be synonymous with evacuate; (D) *disappear* can be synonymous with evaporate.

12. **B** *Deceive* and *mislead* mean the same thing. (A) *Get* is synonymous with receive; (C) *promise*, meaning to pledge or assure, is an antonym; (D) *create* is synonymous with conceive.

13. **D** *Urgent* means needing immediate attention; of the choices given, *important* is closest in meaning. (A) *Tempting* means appealing or enticing; (B) *unnecessary* is an antonym; (C) *professional* means accomplished or skillful.

14. **C** The verb "to temper" means to moderate, toughen, or condition. (A) *Pace* means to walk back and forth or set a tempo; (B) *lure* is to tempt; (D) *feud* is to wage a long-term quarrel.

15. **B** The best synonym for *fastidious* is demanding. The word also means difficult to please or meticulous (concerned with attention to detail). (A) *Rapid-paced* is synonymous with fast, which is not related to fastidious. (C) *Neat* means clean and orderly; (D) *quirky* means peculiar.

16. **A** *Appeal* means to accuse, request, interest, or attract. (B) *Be visible* is synonymous with appear; (C) *calm* is synonymous with appease; (D) *repel* is the opposite of appeal/attract.

17. **B** *Virtuoso* means skillful. (A) *Scholarly* means learned; (C) *kindly* is synonymous with virtuous; (D) *passionate* means enthusiastic or easily angered or lustful.

18. **C** *Inadvertent* means unintentional or thoughtless. (A) *Intentional* is the opposite of inadvertent; (B) *fickle* means erratic, wishy-washy; (D) *whimsical* means unpredictable.

19. **A** To *profess* is to admit, believe, affirm. If you selected (B) *teach*, you were confusing the nouns teacher and professor. (C) *Work* and *profession* are sometimes synonymous, but again, the word is different from profess. All three words—*profess, professor,* and *profession*—come from the same Latin root, which means to declare publicly. (D) *Outline* is synonymous with profile, which is not related.

20. **A** *Reconcile* means to settle or resolve differences. (B) *Praise,* (C) *memorize,* and (D) *rest* are not related in meaning.

21. **C** A *fraud* is an imposter, one who pretends to be something he isn't, a deceiver. (A) a *vandal* destroys or defaces another person's property; (B) an *embezzler,* in effect, steals money or property that was entrusted to him; (D) a *thief* is also one who steals.

22. **C** To *articulate* and *communicate* both involve speaking. Neither articulation nor communication *require* a response, although communication implies a two-way exchange. (A) *Solve* means to find a solution for. (B) *Debate* is also a means of communication, but implies an active or animated discussion or argument, which

sense isn't contained in either the words articulate or communicate. (D) *Consider* means to think about, or weigh options.

23. **D** *Clever* and *shrewd* both mean cunning and intelligent. (A) *Knife-like* could be synonymous with cleaver, a type of knife; (B) *talented* means having an ability or skill. *Shrewdness* sometimes borders on being (C) *dishonest*, but cleverness implies getting what you want with intelligence rather than deceit.

24. **B** *Disprove* means to prove to be wrong, to deny the truth of; deny, therefore, is the best synonym. (A) *Lie* means to tell an untruth; (C) *argue* is a synonym for dispute; (D) *prohibit* means to forbid.

25. **C** *Mediocre* means ordinary, imperfect, or inferior. (A) *Unsuccessful* is not attaining a goal; (B) *healthy* is not at all related; (D) *offensive* means unpleasant or insulting.

26. **B** *Dismal* means uninteresting or depressing. (A) *Spirited* has the opposite meaning; (C) *frightening* is synonymous with dismaying; (D) *weary* means tired.

27. **D** *Undoubtedly* and *certainly* mean the same thing. (A) *Improbably* means not likely; (B) *generally*, meaning usually, is an antonym; (C) *impossibly* means very incapable of happening.

28. **D** A *rival* is a competitor. (A) a *colleague* is a professional associate; (B) a *servant* performs duties for his employer; (C) an *employer* engages the services of workers.

29. **C** *Discriminate* means to distinguish, to perceive the differences of. *Separate* is the only word choice that has a similar meaning. (A) *Persecute* means to harass or annoy, especially because of beliefs; (B) *implicate* is a synonym for incriminate; (D) *doubt* is to question the truth of.

30. **A** *Introspection* comes from the Latin *introspectus*: *intro* meaning inside, *spectus* to look—or self-examination, to examine one's own thoughts and beliefs. (B) *Shyness* is synonymous with introversion; (C) *concentration* is the act of focusing one's attention; (D) *quietness* is the (small) degree of noise or activity.

31. **C** *Amnesia* is a loss of memory; forgetfulness, meaning failure to remember, is the closest in meaning of the word choices given. (A) *Depression* is the state of being sad or inactive;

(B) *sleeplessness* is a synonym for insomnia; (D) a *phobia* is a fear of something.

32. C *Ignorant* means unaware or unknowing, lacking knowledge of something; inexperienced has the closest meaning of the word choices. (A) *Inferior* means lower in status, poor in quality, or below average; (B) *disgraceful* means causing a loss of honor, shameful; (D) *foolish* means absurd or ridiculous.

33. D To *covet* is to enviously desire something. (A) To *shelter*, meaning to protect or cover, can be synonymous with keeping something covert (secret); (B) *steal* is not related; (C) to *promise* may be synonymous with keeping a covenant, or pact.

34. A *Chronic* and *repeat* are synonymous. *Chronic* may also mean long-term. (B) *Painful* is not related, although a chronic condition may also be painful; (C) *acute* means sharp or severe; (D) *brief*, meaning short-term, is an antonym of chronic.

35. D *Deference* means a courteous respect or a yielding of opinion or desire. (A) *Avoidance* is keeping away from; (B) *dissimilarity* is synonymous with difference; (C) *resistance* is a synonym for defiance.

Answers & Explanations

PART 2: PARAGRAPH COMPREHENSION ANSWER KEY

1. B	6. C	11. B
2. D	7. B	12. C
3. A	8. C	13. C
4. B	9. B	14. A
5. D	10. A	15. C

DETAILED ANSWER EXPLANATIONS

1. **B** The writer concludes the paragraphs by stating that honey-gathering methods became widespread, and that commercial beekeeping spread into other states. Spreading is a kind of development. The paragraph shows a development in time from "In the beginning." Even though the writer talks about some of the history of beekeeping, the point is how it developed and spread to other states.

2. **D** Although the victim of Alzheimer's may forget to turn off the oven, the writer says nothing about the victim's disliking any particular food.

3. **A** Since a motivated person generally learns faster, the reader can assume that only (A) can be correct. The writer says nothing about "need" (D) or being "tired" (C), or how they affect the learner. To be unmotivated (B) is just the opposite of what the writer says.

4. **B** The writer discusses "highs" and "lows" of something nearest to or farthest from the moon. The continents do not get higher and lower because the sun and moon are in different positions. Only the water, or oceans, could react in such a way. Also, the sun and moon are bodies that have relative "attractions" for one

another—they do not get higher or lower. Since it is bodies of water—or oceans—that have tides, (B) is the correct answer.

5. **D** The writer states that Newton's theory of universal gravitation was his supreme work. "Most important" is close in meaning to supreme. That it was disputed or misunderstood is never discussed by the writer.

6. **C** Watch out, this is a little tricky. Notice that the studies were of "the satellites" of Jupiter (i.e., the moons of that planet), not of the planet itself; (C) is correct.

7. **B** Solar energy is becoming a logical alternative because of the unavailability of conventional fuels, so (B) must be the answer. The cost of conventional fuels is increasing, so the correct answer can't be (A). Although the writer says solar heating is good for the environment, nothing is mentioned about conventional fuels being good. Conventional fuels (coal, oil, and gas) are much closer than the sun—they are right here on Earth.

8. **C** The writer implies that de Leon only thought his "island" of Florida was an island. The quotation marks around "island" indicate that the word is used not in its true sense. In fact, Florida is an extension—an outward reaching, but connected part—of the mainland of the American continent. Nothing is said about Indians (D) or volcanoes (A). Answer (B) is incorrect; an island is a body of land completely surrounded by water, and since Florida is not completely surrounded by water, it can't be an island.

9. **B** Since the "product" of "conceiving" is (to "produce") foals, and since conceiving happens during breeding, conceiving must mean becoming pregnant. "Producing living foals" is not a sickness (A). Here, producing means giving birth to. Although some animals die giving birth (producing), they do not die while conceiving (C).

10. **A** The writer makes it clear that the young are not educated (a form of caring), because the parents are usually involved with gathering their own food and reproducing.

11. B The writer clearly states that "the label phobia is applied to the person's fear and avoidance." Phobic persons, according to the writer, cannot control their fears. The writer doesn't say anything about how phobics feel about their fears, only that they experience strong reactions.

12. C The topic (T) sentence states that "the health hazard of asbestos fibers" is what makes it a controversial building material.

13. C The passage states that the "stars have been relied upon" by travelers and others. Since "relied upon" and "depended upon" mean virtually the same thing, the passage is telling us that man has depended on stars at times—and (C) is the correct answer.

14. A Nothing was said about interviews with inhabitants in the paragraph.

15. C The passage states, "The mollusk covers the irritant with a substance called nacre." Man doesn't do it—the mollusk does. Consequently, the reader can assume that the mollusk must produce this substance naturally, or "organically," to cover any irritant in its system—artificially implanted by man or not.

Answers & Explanations

1. A	10. D	19. B
2. D	11. C	20. C
3. C	12. B	21. D
4. C	13. D	22. B
5. D	14. A	23. C
6. D	15. B	24. A
7. B	16. D	25. D
8. B	17. A	
9. A	18. B	

DETAILED ANSWER EXPLANATIONS

1. **A** The answer is (A) because the third angle equals $180° - 90° - 70° = 20°$ since it is a right triangle.

2. **D** The answer is (D) because $14 \times 14 = 196$.

3. **C** The answer is (C) because dividing by -6 (and reversing the direction of the inequality) gives $x < 2$.

4. **C** The answer is (C) because the perimeter equals 12 inches or each side equals 3 inches and the area is equal to $s^2 = 3 \times 3 = 9$.

5. **D** The answer is (D) because $(x - 2)(x - 3) = x^2 - 3x - 2x + 6 = x^2 - 5x + 6$.

6. **D** The answer is (D) because the perimeter equals 2 times the length plus 2 times the width. The length is equal to 2 times the width or $2w$. Therefore, the equation is $6w = 24$.

7. B The answer is (B) because the total freshman class times .40 equals 200 or 200/.40 = 500 students in the freshman class.

8. B The answer is (B) because dividing by −10 (and reversing the direction of the inequality) gives $x \leq -6.5$.

9. A The answer is (A) because using the Pythagorean Theorem and letting l be the other leg, $6^2 + l^2 = 10^2$ (because one-half foot equals 6 inches). Then $36 + l^2 = 100$, or $l^2 = 64$. The other leg equals 8 inches.

10. D The answer is (D) because $(9 \times 2) - 26 = -8$.

11. C The answer is (C) because $(z + 4)(z - 5) = z^2 - 5z + 4z - 20 = z^2 - z - 20$.

12. B The answer is (B) because a pentagon has five sides.

13. D The answer is (D) because 75% or .75 times 60 play only basketball, or $.75 \times 60 = 45$.

14. A The answer is (A) because the area of the circle is equal to twice the circumference or $2(2\pi r) = \pi r^2$, or $4r = r^2$. Since r cannot equal 0, $r = 4$.

15. B The answer is (B) because multiplying by −3 (and reversing the direction of the inequality) gives $x < -12$.

16. D The answer is (D) because factoring $v^2 - 2v - 15$ gives $(v + 3)(v - 5)$.

17. A The answer is (A) because the perimeter of a square equals $4s$ and the perimeter of a rectangle equals 2 times the length and 2 times the width or $4s = 8 + 2l$.

18. B The answer is (B) because Jane reads a total of 50 pages in the five nights and this is 40% or .40 of the total assignment. Total assignment = 50/.40 = 125.

19. B The answer is (B) because the two angles formed by the hypotenuse must add up to 90°. The angle which is not given must be 90° − 25°= 65°. Therefore, the difference between these two angles is 65° − 25° = 40°.

20. C The answer is (C) because $(w + 6)(w + 2) = w^2 + 2w + 6w + 12 = w^2 + 8w + 12$.

21. **D** The answer is (D) because the final selling cost = $1.20 + .45(1.20)$ = $\$1.74$.

22. **B** The answer is (B) because there are two equal angles in an isosceles triangle.

23. **C** The answer is (C) because $13 \times 13 = 169$.

24. **A** The answer is (A) because $(4 \times 3) + 12 = 24$.

25. **D** The answer is (D) because $s^2 = 2(4s)$ or $s^2 = 8s$. Since s cannot equal 0, then $s = 8$.

Answers & Explanations

PART 4: ARITHMETIC REASONING ANSWER KEY

1. C	11. C	21. C
2. D	12. D	22. D
3. A	13. B	23. B
4. D	14. A	24. A
5. B	15. C	25. C
6. A	16. D	26. D
7. C	17. B	27. C
8. D	18. A	28. A
9. B	19. C	29. C
10. A	20. A	30. C

DETAILED ANSWER EXPLANATIONS

1. **C** The answer is (C) because $7 \times 89 = 623$¢, or $6.23.

2. **D** The answer is (D) because 28% of $35,000 is $9,800.

3. **A** The answer is (A) because the lion is gaining on the zebra at a rate of 10 miles per hour. He has a quarter mile to go, and each mile takes one-tenth of an hour, or six minutes. Thus, the quarter of a mile will take a quarter of six minutes, or 1.5 minutes.

4. **D** The answer is (D) because the savings account pays 5% of $1,000, or $50, and the CD pays 6% of $2,000, or $120. Thus, the total interest is $170.

5. **B** The answer is (B) because $155,000 − $120,000 = $35,000.

6. **A** The answer is (A) because $500 − 68 + 43 = 475$.

7. **C** The answer is (C) because $6 \times 3 = 18$.

8. **D** The answer is (D) because 12/4 = 3.

9. **B** The answer is (B) because 13.5/2 = 6.75.

10. **A** The answer is (A) because at 40 miles per hour the trip will take her four hours. She left at 8:00, so she will arrive at 12:00.

11. **C** The answer is (C) because 136/8.5 = 16.

12. **D** The answer is (D) because half of the 12 dancers are females, making six females. Half of those, or three of them, were wearing black.

13. **B** The answer is (B) because time and a half would be 1.5 × $12/hour = $18/hour. Working two hours, she would earn 2 × $18 = $36.

14. **A** The answer is (A) because the car gets 30 miles to the gallon, and each gallon costs $1.29. So it costs $1.29 to drive 30 miles. Driving 20 miles would cost $1.29 × (20/30), or $0.86.

15. **C** The answer is (C) because $7 − $3.58 = $3.42.

16. **D** The answer is (D) because 21 + 16 + 13 = 50.

17. **B** The answer is (B) because Brian needs 21 − 17 = 4 more goals. He has two games in which to score four goals, so he would need to average 4/2 = 2 goals per game.

18. **A** The answer is (A) because 6 × 4 = 24.

19. **C** The answer is (C) because 7 × 24 = 168.

20. **A** The answer is (A) because the boat will travel 20 − 5 = 15 miles per hour against the wind. At this rate it will take 30/15 = 2 hours to travel 30 miles.

21. **C** The answer is (C) because there are 4 × 16 = 64 defenders in the league. If three of them make the all-star team, then 64 − 3 = 61 will not.

22. **D** The answer is (D) because the 100% markup will bring the price to 20¢. Then 10% tax is 2¢, so the total is 22¢.

23. **B** The answer is (B) because 24 towels is enough for 24/2 = 12 sets, and 31 washcloths is enough for 31/3 = 10.3, or 10, sets. There will be 10 complete sets, consisting of 20 towels and 30 washcloths, and four extra towels and one extra washcloth.

24. A The answer is (A) because from 8:30 to 12:00 is 3.5 hours. From 12:00 to 5:15 is 5.25 hours. The total is 8.75 hours. But then subtract 45 minutes, or 0.75 hour, for lunch. She worked eight hours.

25. C The answer is (C) because 68 − (−24) = 68 + 24 = 92 degrees.

26. D The answer is (D) because there are 300 male freshmen, hence 600 freshmen. Then there are 1,200 seniors, and half of them, or 600, are females.

27. C The answer is (C) because 80 × 7 = 560.

28. A The answer is (A) because 100% − 60% = 40% of the 30 were incomplete. But 40% of 30 is 12.

29. C The answer is (C) because 74 − 16 − 12 − 29 = 17.

30. C The answer is (C) because (24 + 21 + 13 + 17 + 15)/5 = 90/5 = 18.

Index

Notes

Notes